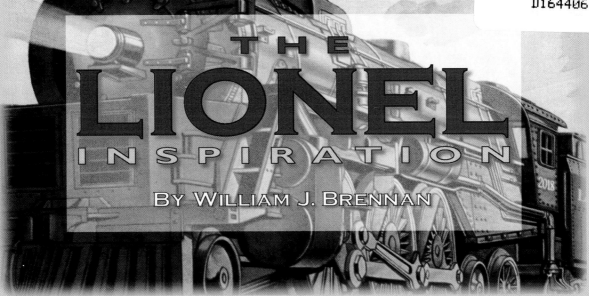

THE LIONEL INSPIRATION

By William J. Brennan

Hudson 5358 speeds Train 23 westbound
through Dearborn, Michigan in June 1940.
(Emery J. Gulash photo)

Lionel's masterpiece steam locomotive, the 700E,
was being manufactured simultaneously from
1937 to 1942. *(William J. Brennan collection)*

Published by
Morning Sun Books, Inc.
9 Pheasant Lane
Scotch Plains, NJ 07076

Library of Congress
Catalog Card No. 97-070600

First Printing
ISBN 1-878887-76-9

Color separation and printing by
The Kutztown Publishing Co., Inc.
Kutztown, Pennsylvania

Dedication

to BARBARA, BONNIE AND BILLY

Acknowledgements

Assembling this book without the contributions of skilled photographers who shared my interest in the model and toy trains produced by the Lionel Corporation and the prototype railroad equipment that inspired their production, would not be possible. In this regard, we commend them for what they added to this endeavor; namely Robert J. Yanosey of Morning Sun Books, John E. Henderson, Jay Duke, Max Knoecklein, Otto Schade and many other members of the Train Collectors Association with important information on the trains that captured our imaginations, real and Lionel models. Bob Yanosey conceived the concept for this book more than ten years ago. Together, my friend and I have been able to bring this long-term project to the beautiful book you see before you.

The patience of my wife, daughter and son, tolerating my monopolizing of the family room with the computer, printouts and piles of books and Lionel catalogues was also essential to the completion of this work and is really appreciated.

Table of Contents

THE LIONEL INSPIRATION

BY WILLIAM J. BRENNAN

From its earliest forms to the most modern equipment used in the United States or elsewhere in the world, the railroad attracted interest in many ways. The afficianados of the industry took photographs, wrote or purchased books, collected timetables and other souvenirs or collected models of the varied creations that roamed on steel rails. In more recent years, those interested in recording the passing railroad scene took black and white photos, color slides and movies to preserve the images of trains that would some day change or vanish completely. Others chose to preserve the memories of their favorite railroad equipment in the form of scale models in a wide range of sizes and track gauges. Still others collected the mass produced toy trains manufactured by Lionel, American Flyer and others that were purchased by most of their original owners as playthings for children.

A substantial number of model railroaders entered the hobby as adolescents or adults, directly with the purchase of "HO" or other scale model trains. However, a greater number manifested their love of model trains at a more tender age, like five to seven years, under a Christmas tree. While many of the early toy or "tinplate" trains bore small resemblance to anything that traversed real railroad tracks, many examples of later production would prove appealing to those whose railroad interests spanned both the photographic and train collecting aspects of this fascinating hobby. The author is just such a hobbyist who extensively photographed American railroads from the 1950's to date and also acquired a substantial collection of those Lionel trains that closely resembled scale models. Such resemblance, of course, must allow for the realities of production economics and the need for these trains to negotiate sharp curves such as on ovals around Christmas trees, that, in proportion to real railroads, would be found only on street car lines or rapid transit systems. Still, seeing a New York Central Hudson, a Western Pacific F3, a Lackawanna Train Master or the Pennsylvania's GG1 powered CONGRESSIONAL navigate a modest circuit of Lionel "O" gauge track in one's basement or den, captured enough of the essence of the prototype to make the acquisitions worth the effort. The rugged construction and sound design of Lionel trains assured reliable operation and this, too, contributed to a realistic effect.

I hope that reading this book, *The Lionel Inspiration* presents a linkage between two of the most fascinating aspects of the railroad hobby. Both railfans and train collectors will be surprised that many of Lionel's products were far more accurate copies of their prototypes than one might expect from a toy manufacturer. To the Lionel train collector, one could paraphrase the old Christmas saying: "Yes, Virginia, there actually were real trains that looked like many of those Lionel creations."

TIME LINE

PROTOTYPE

LIONEL TRAINS

Year	Prototype	Lionel Trains
1901		First Lionel electric trains are made in 2 7/8" gauge.
1902	Pennsylvania's first B6 0-6-0 switcher is built. Similar locomotives were built up to 1926 and one remained in service until 1959.	
1904	First New York Central "S Motor" enters service.	
1911		Lionel introduces its 1911 Special (similar to No. 42.) patterned after the "S Motor"
1927	First New York Central "Hudson" is built by the American Locomotive Co.	
1934	Union Pacific's streamliner "M10000" begins its 65 city tour.	Lionel No. 752E streamliner appears in the company's catalog and begins the "O72" line.
1934	New York Central streamlines "Hudson" 5344 with the name *Commodore Vanderbilt*.	Lionel follows suit with its No. 264 and No. 265 "O" gauge versions.
1934	The first Pennsylvania GG-1 is built with a riveted body. The smooth welded version followed in 1935.	
1935	Milwaukee Road's HIAWATHA Atlantic enters service.	Lionel introduces its No. 250E semi-scale HIAWATHA in "O72".
1935	Boston & Maine places its FLYING YANKEE in Boston- Portland service.	Lionel produces its No. 616 "O" gauge FLYING YANKEE.
1936	The CITY OF DENVER streamliner begins revenue service on the Union Pacific.	The "O" gauge CITY OF DENVER appears in the Lionel catalog.
1937		The scale model "Hudson" No. 700EW tops the Lionel "O" gauge line.
1939	General Motors introduces its FT road diesel and NW2 switcher.	Lionel introduces its No. 708 scale model Pennsylvania B6 0-6-0 switcher in full scale "O72" with semi-scale companions including No. 227.
1941	Norfolk & Western builds its first class J streamlined 4-8-4 passenger locomotive.	
1942	The Pennsylvania builds its first futuristic N5C cabin car with porthole windows.	
1944	Baldwin Locomotive Works completes Pennsylvania's S2 direct drive steam turbine 6-8-6.	
1946		Lionel's No. 671 and No. 2020 appear as revolutionary 20 wheel turbines in "O" and "O27" freight and passenger sets.
1946	General Motors' EMD division resumes diesel switcher production that was interrupted in 1942 including the 1000 hp. NW2 in its postwar line.	

PROTOTYPE

LIONEL TRAINS

	PROTOTYPE	LIONEL TRAINS
1947		Pennsylvania's GG1 electric is introduced by Lionel, its first model of an electric locomotive since 1936.
1948	Electro-Motive offers its versatile Phase III F3 dual service road diesel.	Lionel brings out a close to scale model of the F3 2333 in Santa Fe or New York Central colors.
1949	Electro-Motive introduces its 1500 hp F7 featuring an improved electrical system	The NW2 appears as No. 622 and No. 6220 in Santa Fe black with a ringing bell and the first version of Magne Traction™.
1949	The GP7 enters the market as the first successful road switcher produced by Electro-Motive.	
1950	The stainless steel self-propelled Rail Diesel Car (RDC) is introduced by the Budd Co. of Philadelphia.	
1950	American Locomotive Co. (Alco) introduces its 1600 hp. FA-2 freight diesel cab units.	An "O27" likeness of the Alco appears in Union Pacific paint with Magne-Traction in the 1950 Lionel catalog.
1953		The distinctive Pennsylvania N5C cabin car appears in the Lionel catalog as No. 6417.
1953	Fairbanks-Morse's massive 2400 hp. Train Master tours a number of railroads to generate sales.	
1954		Lionel introduces No. 2321, a Lackawanna Train Master, its most powerful diesel model.
1954	Electro-Motive raises the horsepower of its best-selling road switcher from 1500 to 1750 and designates the new model as GP9.	
1955		The GP7 appears in the Lionel catalog in Pennsylvania, Burlington and Milwaukee colors.
1955	General Electric delivers ten colorful 4000 hp. EP-5 electric locomotives to the New Haven.	
1956	Virginian's 3300 hp. EL-C rectifier electrics are delivered by General Electric.	
1956	Baldwin-Lima-Hamilton builds its last new locomotive	Lionel introduces its No. 400 Budd RDC-1 as a powered coach.
1956		No. 2350 represents the New Haven EP-5 in the Lionel catalog.
1957		The Norfolk & Western "J" appears in the Lionel catalog as its No. 746.
1958	Fairbanks-Morse exits U.S. locomotive market	Lionel offers a shortened version of the Virginian rectifier locomotive as No. 2329.
1958		By adding a dynamic brake housing to the roof of its GP7, Lionel creates its "GP9" which first appears in M&StL colors as No. 2348.

ELECTRIC LOCOMOTIVES

THE
NEW YORK
CENTRAL
"S" MOTOR

The first of this famous class of electric passenger locomotives was completed on October 27, 1904 through the combined efforts of the American Locomotive Company and the General Electric Company, both of Schenectady, New York. Initially carrying the number 6000, the first "S" motor was 37 feet long, weighed about 100 tons and was powered by four 550 hp direct current motors. For nearly two years, the locomotive was tested on six miles of temporarily electrified trackage west of Schenectady and racked up 50,000 miles in the process. A total of 47 of these compact electrics appeared on the New York Central motive power roster between 1904 and 1909 and, by the 1970's, the survivors qualified as the oldest locomotives operating in America on a Class 1 carrier.

The "S" motors inspired the fledgling electric train manufacturers to produce a number of toy likenesses and they proved to be as popular with the customers of the time as they became in later years with train collectors. Lionel began producing its entries in the toy train market in 1910, fairly soon after the prototypes entered service and continued some models until 1936.

The various Lionel locomotives had cabs that reasonably approximated the "S" motor outline but, because of practical manufacturing economics, shared existing plate motors with other toy locomotives in the Lionel line. The author considers the No. 42 as well as the

1911 and 1912 Specials to be the best early standard gauge examples and the later 402 and 408 the best examples in what many collectors consider to be the "Golden Age"of standard gauge. In 1915 and 1916, Lionel manufactured the No. 703 in "O" gauge and followed with the No. 156 which remained in the catalog from 1917 to 1923.

"S" motor 105 reposes on the inspection pit under Grand Central Terminal in April 1964. *(William J. Brennan photo)*

"S" motor 110 pauses at North White Plains while hauling a special excursion train in October 1966.
(William J. Brennan photo)

The influence of the New York Central "S" motor shows clearly on the Lionel No. 42 electric. The popularity of
prototype side-rodded electric locomotives in 1919 and the opportunity to use existing model steam type motors
probably influenced the choice of drive. *(Joel H. Cane collection)*

Lionel's No. 408 used a modified "S" motor carbody and a rigid frame that more closely resembled the prototype's.
(Joel H. Cane collection)

THE MILWAUKEE ROAD BI-POLARS

By the early 1920's, the Chicago, Milwaukee, St. Paul and Pacific Railroad was operating 656 route miles of electrified mainline trackage across the Rocky and Cascade Mountains. The line traversed some of the most impressive scenery in the country and attracted a substantial portion of the transcontinental passenger traffic. Increasing passenger train weights inspired the design and construction in 1919-1920 of five 265 ton gearless "Bi-polar" electric locomotives for service on the Coast Division. Like the "S" and "T" motors of the New York Central, the armatures were mounted directly on the driving axles. Smooth, nearly silent operation of the powerful 76-foot-long locomotive's 24 driving wheels was the result. Instead of the box-shaped cabs typical of electric locomotives of the period, these consisted of three jointed sections with a rectangular cab at the center, with two semi-cylindrical hoods at the ends.

The Bi-polars could handle passenger trains of 1120 tons over the mountainous routes of both the Rocky Mountain and Coast Divisions. They were originally painted solid black but, with the introduction of the HIAWATHA passenger trains, appeared in an attractive maroon and orange scheme. Their final appearance was Union Pacific yellow and gray to harmonize with the CITY streamliners that the Milwaukee was hauling between Omaha, Nebraska and Chicago. Morning Sun Books shows many color illustrations of the electric operations and other aspects of this fascinating railroad in its volume *Under Milwaukee Wires*. One Bi-polar is preserved in the National Museum of Transport in St. Louis; the other four were scrapped in the 1960's.

(Montague L. Powell photo, Wm. Woelfer Collection)

The notoriety of the Milwaukee Bi-polar inspired Lionel to produce a considerably shortened version in Standard Gauge in 1928 as its No. 381 with twelve wheels. The model locomotive, which captured the essence of the prototype's appearance, was catalogued with the company's top of the line "State" passenger train set, which was offered until 1936. The set was so named because the cars carried the names *Colorado, California, Illinois* and *New York*. The cars were realistically proportioned and quite well detailed, including interiors. In accordance with the company's preference for attractive colors on most of its rolling stock, the 381 was painted dark green instead of the prototype's black.

Two smaller, simpler Standard Gauge locomotives, the No. 10 and No. 380 had similar lines, but were much shorter and had only four wheels. These were catalogued with more economical train sets. Similar looking four-wheeled "O" gauge locomotives also appeared during this period, the No. 4 and No. 254.

The Milwaukee Road

Bi-polar E-3 pauses at Butte, Montana with Train 15, the OLYMPIAN HIAWATHA in May 1958. A 1953 rebuilding included rounding the ends of the hoods as a modest sort of streamlining. *(Montague L. Powell photo, Wm. Woelfer collection)*

The first Bi-polar, E-1 displays its new yellow and gray color scheme in the engine terminal at Deer Lodge, Montana in May 1958. When the Milwaukee Road began handling Union Pacific streamliners between Omaha, Nebraska and Chicago, Illinois, its passenger power was re-painted to match these trains. *(Montague L. Powell photo, Wm. Woelfer collection)*

The highly desirable No. 381 retains the overall appearance of the massive Bi-polar despite the considerable foreshortening necessary for tinplate curves and maintaining a manageable weight for boys to handle. *(Joel H. Cane collection)*

THE PENNSYLVANIA GG1

The Pennsylvania Railroad's GG1 passenger and freight locomotives are widely regarded as the most famous electric motive power in this country and, possibly, the world. The 80-foot-long prototype with its ageless design by Raymond Loewy is considered to be a classic by most railroad historians, model railroaders and train collectors. Mr. Loewy was an extremely innovative industrial designer whose other works include streamlining a Pennsylvania K4 steam locomotive, the Baldwin "Shark Nose" diesel road units and the 1947 Studebaker. (The streamlined K4 was also modeled, in an approximate fashion, by Lionel as its prewar No. 238.) The first GG1, No. 4800, was built in 1935. Its graceful appearance was compromised somewhat by its riveted body construction. Subsequent GG1's had smooth, all-welded bodies, eliminating the esthetic shortcomings of the pioneer unit. The attractiveness of its lines, its reputation for outstanding performance and its high visibility serving the populous "Northeast Corridor" rendered it a "natural" for toy and model train manufacturers to consider. These graceful machines were seen not only by those who lived in the region served by the Pennsy's electrified main lines that connected New York City with Harrisburg, PA. and Washington, D.C., but by many passengers from the South and Midwest whose connecting trains were propelled under the catenary wire by the GG1's.

The real GG1's carried a wide variety of color schemes. During their early years on the Pennsylvania, they were mostly Brunswick Green with the five gold "cat whisker" stripes until the 1950's. When the railroad introduced its new CONGRESSIONAL train with a stainless steel consist, a few of the graceful electrics were painted Tuscan Red with the five gold stripes. By the mid-50's, the GG1's began to appear in the single broad stripe color scheme with the large red keystone and the "Pennsylvania" name spelled out in bold letters on the sides. While most engines were painted in Brunswick Green during this period, a few appeared in a Tuscan Red version planned for CONGRESSIONAL service.

Pennsy Electric Years and *PRR: Hudson to Horseshoe* by Morning Sun Books offers many excellent color illustrations of these electric racehorses in action.

The ensuing years would prove to be unkind to both the Pennsylvania Railroad and the Lionel Corporation. The handsome lines of the real GG1's would be compromised by the stark solid black of their new owner, Penn Central, relieved only by the road name and the "worm" emblem in white. The Lionel Corporation would also face declining sales and steady attrition in its catalogs.

When the national passenger carrier, Amtrak was formed in 1971, it acquired much of the equipment of the private railroads that were previously providing the service. A number of GG1's became Amtrak property for Northeast Corridor service and many were painted in Amtrak colors. During the mid-70's, GG1 No.4935 was restored by Amtrak to its original Pennsy Brunswick Green with the five stripes, through volunteer fund raising.

While a number of manufacturers produced scale models in various gauges, the most popular and best-known versions were produced by the Lionel Corporation in "O" gauge tinplate form. According to Frank Pettit, a retired design engineer who worked for Lionel for 35 years, Joshua Lionel Cowan read a newspaper clipping in 1946, showing a

GG1 4905 brings Lehigh Valley Train 24 into the
turnaround loop at Sunnyside Yard in Long Island
City, New York in July 1953. *(Robert Malinoski photo)*

The Pennsy was justly proud of its GG1
achievement and featured one high above
Philadelphia on the cover of its 1960
Annual Reporrt. *(R.J. Yanosey collection)*

Restored GG1 4935 awaits attention in the Wilmington, Delaware electric shop in May 1977.
The Pennsylvania RR had been merged away nine years prior, when railroad fans were permitted to repaint
this Amtrak-owned GG1 into the classic PRR pin-stripes. *(Bill Volkmer collection)*

photograph of a GG1 and decided that the graceful Pennsy electric should appear in his catalog. The clipping was sent to Joe Bonanno, the company's Chief Engineer, with instructions to begin the design and production process. Within 24 hours, the project was assigned to Mr. Pettit, who promptly contacted the Pennsylvania Railroad to obtain any available information on the GG1. The railroad's public relations department gladly arranged to provide extensive data, including blueprints and a sample of Brunswick Green paint. In 1947, the production version appeared with a shortened body and wheelbase that allowed it to operate smoothly on the tight curves of Lionel's 31-inch-diameter "O" gauge tinplate track. The locomotive, which has been produced in many different forms with varying color schemes and features, remains an attractive, if foreshortened portrayal of its famous prototype.

Many observers compare watching the Lionel model pulling *Madison* cars (short, but well-proportioned standard type Pullmans) or the CONGRESSIONAL set (with the aluminum streamlined cars) to viewing a photograph of a real Pennsy GG1 and train that was taken with a telephoto lens.

Lionel issued its first version of the GG1, No. 2332, in black, and later in green with the five stripes. The black engines, probably reflecting an attempt to simulate the hard-to-reproduce Brunswick Green, are quite rare and, consequently highly desired by collectors; the discrepancy was discovered early in production and the rest of these engines were

painted in a dark green that more closely approximated the Brunswick Green of the real GG1. This model had a single motor, nickel wheel rims and a black plastic klaxon horn whose sound more closely resembled a frog than a locomotive horn. These early 20 wheeled engines had modest pulling power for their size and Lionel would ultimately decide that improvements were in order.

The passenger set that Lionel first sold with the GG1 included three maroon Pullman cars named *Irvington*, *Madison* and *Manhattan*. Despite their Pullman window pattern, these cars bore some resemblance to the Tuscan Red P-70 steel coaches used at the time by the Pennsy. Three car passenger consists appeared behind GG1's regularly on the real railroad's busy electrified mainline on non-rush hour shore trains. Lionel's catalog set suggested just such a train that ran between Penn Station, New York and South Amboy, N. J., where the overhead wire ended and a steam or diesel locomotive took over to bring the train to Point Pleasant and Bay Head Junction.

In 1950, Lionel introduced its "Magne-Traction" model locomotives with Alnico permanent magnets installed either in the axles or in the frame, parallel to the axles and between the drive wheels. Driving wheels were then made of sintered iron so that they could conduct a magnetic field and make the engine hug the track for more pulling power. Engines that were so equipped would also be less likely to roll off the tracks when they rounded curves at high speeds. This improvement appeared that year in the No. 2330

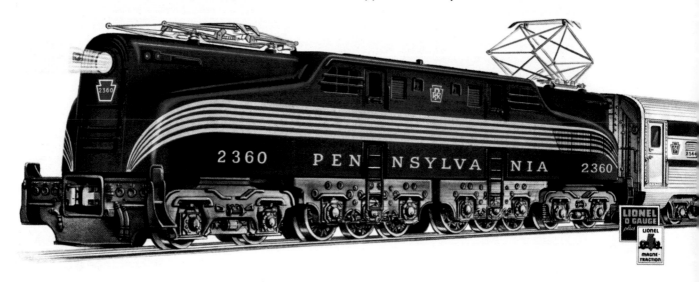

The 105 mm. telephoto lens has shortened the appearance of this northbound train out of Washington, D.C. in October 1967, making GG1 4904 more closely resemble its Lionel counterpart. *(William J. Brennan photo)*

A Budd ad appearing in the *National Geographic* and other major magazines describes the amenities offered by the new stainless steel streamliners, THE MORNING CONGRESSIONAL, THE SENATOR AND THE AFTERNOON CONGRESSIONAL streamliners that brightened up the New York - Washington passenger trade in the early 1950's. Note the appearance of our nation's capitol in this and the photo above. *(R.J. Yanosey collection)*

Pride of the Pennsy . . . The Great Congressional
1956 Lionel Catalog, pages 24-25

GG1, along with twin motors, that greatly enhanced its tractive effort. Operators of these engines could then run the longer trains that would better characterize their powerful prototypes. The 2330 appeared in the same five stripe green color scheme as its predecessor. Its horn was a bicycle buzzer that was activated by a single size "D" flashlight battery through a conventional Lionel direct current-triggered whistle/horn relay. The horn, which would be used in many Lionel diesel and electric engines, would prove to be a mixed blessing. While the sound was somewhat more realistic, the battery would decompose and leak if left in the engine for extended periods. The result would be the "battery rot" that is the bane of Lionel collectors to this day. Imagine the frustration of finding an otherwise pristine Lionel diesel or electric locomotive in its original box and then discovering this malady which might have destroyed much of its collectible value.

The streamlined stainless steel consist of Pennsy's New York-to-Washington CONGRESSIONAL of the early 1950's inspired Lionel to introduce its own version in 1955, adapting the 15 inch long aluminum passenger cars in the 2540 series with maroon letterboard stripes and the "Pennsylvania" name spelled out in gold letters. The train was pulled by a GG1 in Tuscan Red with the five stripes, No. 2340. This engine was mechanically identical to the 2330 and had ample power to handle Lionel's CONGRESSIONAL as capably as its prototype on the Pennsylvania's mainline to the nation's Capital. The train was a fairly realistic representation of the real CONGRESSIONAL, except that it included a "Vista Dome" car; the Pennsy did not own such cars. The clearances under its wires, particularly in the Hudson and East River tunnels and in Penn Station were too low for dome cars.

During these years, Lionel also offered a model of the Pennsylvania's N5c porthole-windowed steel caboose in nearly scale size and correct colors and lettering. With an assortment of contemporary Lionel freight cars, this enabled Lionel GG1 owners to assemble a fairly realistic Pennsy freight train of the period. The next color scheme variation of the GG1 appeared in 1957 with the 2360 in Tuscan Red with the contemporary broad stripe color scheme. It, too was mechanically identical to the 2330 and was the final version to be made by the Lionel Corporation at the New Jersey factory in 1963.

The illustration from page 15 of the 1947 Lionel catalog shows how well that the company reproduced a short Pennsylvania GG1-hauled passenger train. Such a train was typical of New York-Philadelphia "clocker" service or NY&LB seashore trains.

The 1950's contemporary look of the prototype GG1 is reproduced quite well in Lionel's broad striped No. 2360.
The broad stripe was PRR's up-to-date look introduced in the mid fifties together with the much larger red keystone.
(William J. Brennan collection)

The resemblance between Lionel's No. 2360 and prototype GG1 4916 at Trenton, New Jersey
in January 1966, is quite clear as this photo shows. *(Matthew J. Herson, Jr. photo)*

THE PENNSYLVANIA RAILROAD CO.

PUBLIC COACH AND PULLMAN TRAIN W-1   Returning

ARMY-NAVY FOOTBALL GAME

PHILADELPHIA (Municipal Stadium), PA. To

SATURDAY, NOVEMBER 26, 1955

Train leaves 10 minutes after the game, from same track on which it arrived.

Non-Transferable.   Subject to tariff regulations.

Form SX 55021-1

GG1 4872 speeds Atlantic Coast Line's EAST COAST CHAMPION toward Washington, D.C. on April 10, 1954. The GG1 and other PRR electrics typically ran with its front pantograph down on the theory that a rear pan/catenary entanglement would allow the rear pan to be pulled down and have the undamaged front pan ahead of and clear of any damage. Generally one would see GG1s running with both pans up only during sleet and snow storms. *(Don Ball collection)*

The Army-Navy Game was a gathering place for GG1s and the 56th annual game was no exception. The Pennsylvania Railroad gave passengers attending the game on November 26, 1955 commemorative picture ticket stubs like this. *(Robert J. Yanosey collection)*

The PENN-HARRISBURG EXPRESS enters the station at Princeton Junction on February 14, 1953. *(Don Ball collection)*

Three GG1's haul a long freight train along the Susquehanna River through beautiful scenery at Safe Harbor, Pennsylvania in1963. As the PRR began to trim its passenger operations in the 1960's, more and more GG1s found employment in the freight pool. *(Don Ball collection)*

EAST-WEST TIME TABLES

PENNSYLVANIA RAILROAD

Issued March 15, 1946

Transportation Progress 1946

The Pennsylvania Railroad's East-West time table of 1946 shows artwork that strongly resembles that of Lionel's catalogs of the late 1940's. *(Robert J. Yanosey collection)*

GG1 4846 and an equally grimy companion roll along the main line with a long string of gondolas in 1962. Freight electric locomotives rarely enjoyed the luxury of going through automatic washers like passenger power. *(Don Ball collection)*

THE
NEW HAVEN
EP-5

In 1954, The New York, New Haven & Hartford Railroad took delivery of ten 4000 h.p. ignitron rectifier electric passenger locomotives numbered 370-379 from the General Electric Company at Erie, Pennsylvania. These units were able to use the railroad's 11,000 volt alternating current (a.c.) overhead catenary wire for their power source while equipped with the highly efficient 600 volt direct current (d.c.) traction motors that proved so successful and economic to manufacture with diesel-electrics. The ignitron rectifiers used Mercury-Arc Tubes in which a continuous arc converted the alternating current to direct current for the traction motors. This process generated a large quantity of heat in a relatively small space so high speed blowers were necessary to provide a sufficient airflow to dissipate the heat and maintain a safe temperature. The blower system emitted a high pitched roar much like jet aircraft; this soon caused these engines to acquire the nickname "Jets", among others.

The EP-5's introduced a double ended car body that was similar in appearance to the postwar Alco diesel-electrics. Ray Patten of General Electric, who designed the handsome Alco freight (FA) and passenger (PA) road diesel bodies, created the lines of these modern electrics. With these engines, the New Haven's new chairman, Patrick B. McGinnis, introduced the first of the eye-catching color schemes composed of contrasting vermilion (reddish orange), black and white geometric shapes, designed by Herbert Matter of Knoll

Associates, reportedly at the inspiration of the chairman's wife, Lucille. Variations of these "McGinnis" color schemes would appear on many New Haven locomotives and freight and passenger cars and later, in black, white and blue on the Boston & Maine Railroad.

The visual and auditory impact of the EP-5's was in stark contrast to the dignified dark Hunter Green with yellow stripes and lettering and relatively quiet operation that generally characterized the New Haven's older electric locomotives. Additional nicknames like "Striped Beasts" and "Screaming Eagles" ensued, apparently in reaction to the sights and sounds of these machines.

The Pennsylvania and New Haven railroads operated through passenger trains like the COLONIAL, SENATOR and PATRIOT between Boston, Massachusetts and Washington, D.C. and exchanged locomotives at Penn Station in New York City, where, during the 1950's and 60's, Pennsylvania GG-1's took the trains southward and the New Haven

EP-5 handled them northward to New England. It was reported to be the only location in the world where a train regularly exchanged one electric locomotive for another.

After 1969, when the New Haven was merged into the Penn Central system, several of the EP-5's received the somber black PC color scheme with the white "intertwined worms" logo. Only two of these rectifiers would survive on the active roster into Conrail in 1976 (but never received any Conrail paint or markings).

Two years after the EP-5's appeared on the New Haven, Lionel introduced its version, catalog No. 2350 which, with some artistic license, was a fairly realistic model. The carbody was quite an accurate reproduction, reflecting only a slight shortening to accommodate the curvature of "O" gauge track. In the interest of production economics, Lionel used the contemporary vertical motored F3 power truck and companion trailer truck, instead of the six-wheel trucks of the proto-

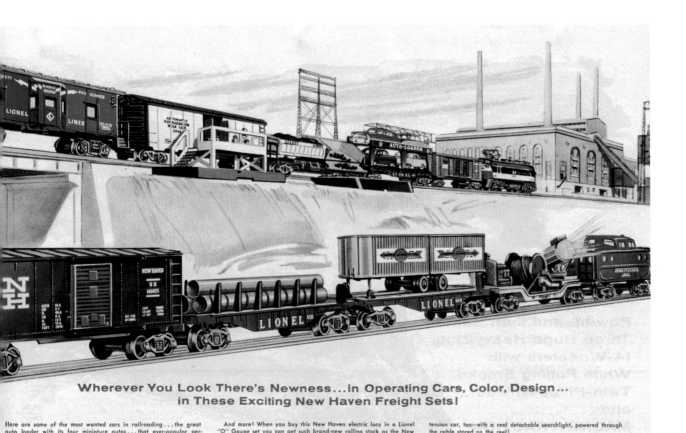

**Wherever You Look There's Newness . . . in Operating Cars, Color, Design . . .
in These Exciting New Haven Freight Sets!**

Here are some of the most wanted cars in railroading . . . the great auto loader with its four miniature autos . . . that ever-popular performer, the operating twin-dump car . . . the long, fun-packed operating milk car . . . the unusual bay window caboose!

And more! When you buy this New Haven electric loco in a Lionel "O" Gauge set you can get such brand-new rolling stock as the New Haven automobile car, the New Haven box car, the 2-van Cooper-Jarrett trailer car! Yes, and the amazing new operating searchlight ex-

tension car, too—with a real detachable searchlight, powered through the cable stored on the reel!

You'll be proud of your New Haven freight set . . . whichever you pick! Be sure to ask your dealer for his low, complete outfit prices!

All Lionel locomotives and cars are a better buy when you purchase them in sets. With "O" sets you get locomotive, cars, track, remote control section, lockon, lubricant and instructions. Ask your Lionel dealer about his complete assortment of "O" outfits, starting as low as $39.95.

19

On a sunny June day in 1962, New Haven's 376 brings the Washington-bound
SENATOR through the south portal of Hell Gate Bridge,
which carries the railroad from the Bronx to Queens. *(William J. Brennan photo)*

New Haven's September 24, 1939 time table illustrates
the company's pride in the impressive Hell Gate Bridge.
(Robert J. Yanosey collection)

The magnificent engineering landmark, the Hell Gate Bridge, connected the boroughs of the Bronx and Queens and made
through Boston-Washington rail service possible. The span was 40 years old when this photo was taken in the spring of
1957. Lionel's No. 300 bridge captured the essence of the prototype and is a prized collectible accessory *(Al Holtz)*

type. Apparently, the EP-5 was not planned for sets with four or more of the 2500 series aluminum passenger cars or a second power truck would have been installed to provide the requisite pulling power. The author often ran this locomotive, as produced, in one of its prototype roles, pulling a miniature version of the mail and express train, the HELL GATE which, in the 1960's preceded the noontime COLONIAL over Hell Gate Bridge on its run between Boston and Washington with a mixture of four or five express refrigerator and Pennsylvania Railroad X-29 boxcars (the prototype cars in this service were equipped with steam and communications lines like passenger cars), with a single CONGRESSIONAL aluminum passenger car. The light plastic and wood bodies of the "express" cars and well-lubricated trucks kept the train within the pulling power of the single motored unit.

Lionel introduced later versions of this unit in color schemes of railroads that had locomotives bearing only distant resemblance to the EP-5. This might have reflected the desire to utilize the tooling for the body style of a highly specific regional design and adapt it to recognizable likenesses of electric locomotives in other parts of the country. The first of the "spin-offs" was the Milwaukee Road version, catalog No. 2351 appearing in 1957. The real-life Milwaukee Road had much larger double cab electric locomotives that ran on chassis that resembled the Pennsylvania's GG-1, but with eight wheel power trucks. These electrics were originally built by General Electric as part of planned postwar aid for the Soviet Union after World War II. When difficulties arose between our countries, some of the locomotives were "reallocated" and were available for sale to the Milwaukee Road and the Chicago, South Shore and South Bend

Railroad. With a nickname inspired by Josef Stalin, the engines were called "Little Joes". The Lionel version was painted yellow with a black upper body and a broad maroon stripe along the slides. By comparison, the Milwaukee Road used orange as a base body color. In 1958, the next variation on the EP-5 theme carried Pennsylvania lettering but it bore little resemblance to any particular locomotive owned by that railroad. The Pennsylvania Railroad had, at the time, four alternating current experimental freight locomotives built by G.E. with similar noses, but these were single cab units that somewhat resembled Alco FA freight diesels in outward appearance. They were painted in Brunswick Green with a single narrow stripe down the sides like the Pennsylvania's freight diesels of the time, contrasting with the adapted broad stripe GG-1 style color scheme used on the Lionel No. 2352.

The final color scheme in which the double cab rectifier appeared was the attractive green and orange of the Great Northern Railway. No. 2358 appeared in 1959 and, like its Milwaukee Road counterpart, bore only a superficial resemblance to the massive electric locomotives that ran between Wenatchee and Skykomish, Washington, pulling freight and pasenger trains through the 7.79 mile long Cascade Tunnel, where potential smoke problems prohibited the use of steam locomotives. The Great Northern had a number of 11,000 volt alternating current engines that strongly resembled the Milwaukee's "Little Joes" in size, wheel arrangement and overall appearance. The prototype electrics were retired from service in 1956 when that region of the railroad was completely dieselized and the new motive power could easily operate through the tunnel.

When the Lionel line of trains was revived by MPC, the EP-5 reappeared in Milwaukee, Pennsylvania and Great Northern liveries.

Sister EP-5's 379 and 374 await their next assignments in the daylight between
Ninth and Tenth Avenues west of New York's Penn Station in April 1968. From this angle, the success of
Lionel's efforts to reproduce the overall appearance of the prototype, is quite evident. *(William J. Brennan collection)*

The Lionel No. 2350 is a fairly close approximation of its colorful prototype, allowing for the realities
of toy train production economics. *(William J. Brennan collection)*

New Haven 370 awaits its next assignment at New Haven, Connecticut in November 1963. *(Don Ball collection)*

EP-5 370 has an FL9 in tow as it threads its way across the switchwork at New Haven, Connecticut, the east end of the railroad's electrification. The New Haven had the unique problem of entering New York City under two different electrification systems: PRR's overhead catenary in Penn Station and NYC's third rail in Grand Central Terminal. *(Don Ball collection)*

Milwaukee Road "Little Joe" E-72 posed for the camera at Deer Lodge, Montana on May 6, 1961 in the color scheme that inspired Lionel's No. 2351. The maroon and orange paint scheme most approximated Lionel's. (Robert J. Yanosey collection)

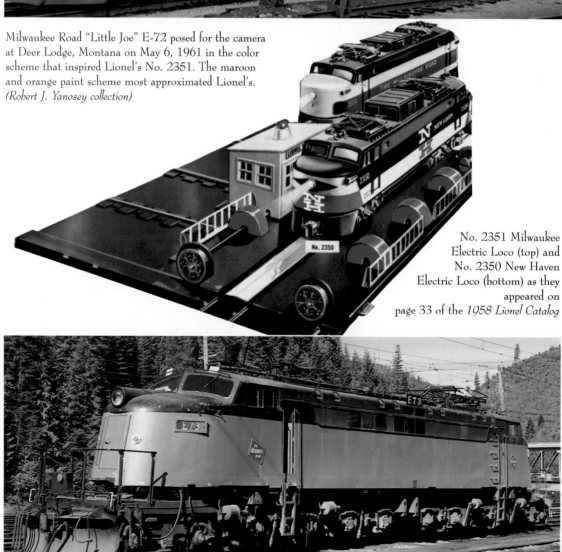

No. 2351 Milwaukee Electric Loco (top) and No. 2350 New Haven Electric Loco (bottom) as they appeared on page 33 of the 1958 Lionel Catalog

Milwaukee Road "Little Joe" E-73 awaits its next assignment at Avery, Idaho on June 4, 1973, illustrating the railroad's later simplified color scheme. Avery was the western end of the Rocky Mountain electrification. The end was near in a time frame for the electrification, which was terminated a year later on June 15, 1974. (Montague L. Powell photo, Wm. Woelfer collection)

In 1950, the Milwaukee Road bought twelve "Little Joes" from General Electric to supplement 1915-17 vintage box cab electrics like E-54, seen here at Deer Lodge, Montana in April 1958. The new units were built in 1948-49 and intended for sale to the Soviet Union but, after the 1948 Berlin Blockade, sales of strategic materials like locomotives were banned. *(Montague L. Powell photo, Wm. Woelfer collection)*

Two of Milwaukee's Little Joes (E20 and E21) were specifically equipped for passenger service. Like many other railroads, the Milwaukee Road promoted its premier passenger trains on matchbooks which were given to passengers. Hopefully the users provided subtle but frequent mini-advertisements for the famous HIAWATHAS. *(Robert J. Yanosey collection)*

CLOSE COVER BEFORE STRIKING

THE MILWAUKEE ROAD

OUT IN FRONT!

ROUTE OF THE *Hiawathas*

The ten freight "Little Joes" (E70-E79) were more often photographed. Here, E-72 leads three diesel units through magnificent Rocky Mountain scenery near Avery, Idaho in November 1972. Alas, all Milwaukee electric service would disappear two years later in 1974 as would the railroad itself eleven years later. *(Tom Brown photo, Wm. Woelfer collection)*

By the 1950's, the Pennsylvania Railroad's fleet of P5a box cab electrics, built in 1932, were reaching the point where replacements would soon be needed. P5a 4758 exemplified the class as it posed in Philadelphia on December 30, 1956. *(Joe Leo photo, Lou Schmitz collection)*

Eager to produce a PRR "Little Joe", Lionel featured the handsome 2352 on *page 32* of its *1958 catalog*.

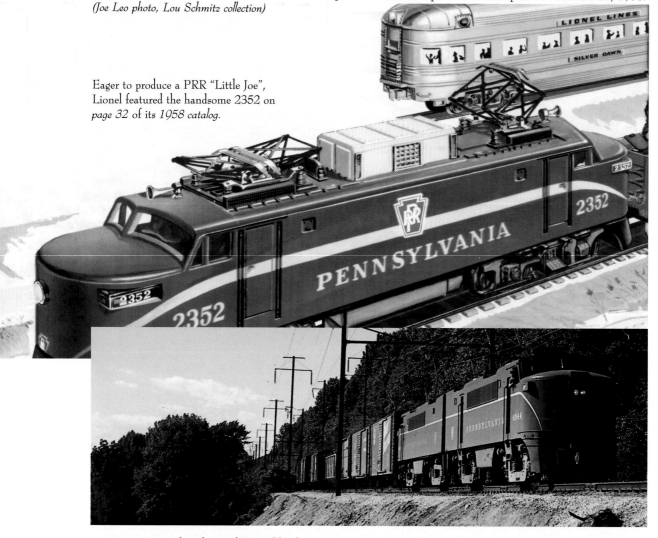

PRR never purchased any of EP5's like the New Haven or any surplus "Little Joes". Instead they asked several builders for prototypes for eventual replacement of its aging P5 fleet. Pennsylvania Railroad's class E2b was one of several competitive builders' bids to replace the P5a fleet. No. 4944 (a General Electric product) leads a sister unit on the road's Atglen & Susquehanna line in 1961. *(James P. Shuman photo)*

E2b 4939 leads two identical units downgrade, generating substantial brake shoe smoke on May 20, 1962. *(James P. Shuman photo)*

Beside GE, Baldwin-Westinghouse also produced cab unit-type electrics for the PRR which somewhat resembled the Lionel 2352. The 4996 was an E3b (at Enola June 11, 1962) while the 4997 was an E2c (also at Enola February 19, 1961). They differed in their trucks. The E3b (4995-4996) had three B-type trucks while the E2c (4997-4998) had two C-type trucks. *(Both, Bill Volkmer)*

THE VIRGINIAN RECTIFIER

The Virginian Railway was primarily a coal-hauling line running from Sewell's Point in Norfolk, Virginia 436 miles westward to Deepwater, about 30 miles southeast of Charleston, West Virginia. Because of the mountainous terrain through which it ran, 134 miles of the railroad were electrified between Roanoke, Virginia and Mullens, West Virginia with an 11,000 volt 25 cycle alternating current system, similar to those of the Pennsylvania and the New Haven railroads. Between October 1956 and February 1957, the Virginian Railway took delivery on twelve new ignitron rectifier electric freight locomotives from General Electric to replace aging side-rodded box cab electrics that dated from 1925-26. The Class EL-C's came in an attractive color scheme of black with yellow striping and the Virginian name in "billboard" lettering on their sides. One critic, however, described them as having "the beauty of misshapen bricks." Most newly styled locomotives receive mixed reviews about their appearance, but gradually achieve acceptance with time. These units proved to be quite reliable in handling the long coal trains over the mountains. They would see four more owners in their careers, mainly because of railroad mergers.

In 1959, the Virginian was purchased by its larger competitor, the Norfolk and Western Railway. The two lines paralleled each other through the Blue Ridge Mountains.

Understandably, the merger partners eliminated redundant trackage to reduce taxes, maintenance and other expenses; most of the Virginian's electrified route would either be abandoned or have too little traffic to justify the cost of maintaining the electric power system. Thus, electric operations ceased in June 1962. This resulted in the older electric locomotives being scrapped and the nearly new rectifiers sold to the New Haven Railroad at $20,000 each, clearly a bargain price.

The New Haven revived its electrified freight operations with the twelve ex-Virginian locomotives which it classified as EF-4's and painted in an attractive orange color scheme with white striping and black lettering.

In 1969, the New Haven Railroad was itself merged into the Penn Central Railroad and its locomotives soon acquired new road numbers and the standard PC black paint with a white "worm" logo and road name. The EF-4 rectifier electrics became class E-33 on the PC and entered the freight electric locomotive pool of ex-Pennsylvania Railroad GG-1's and E-44's operating out of Meadows Yard in Kearny, New Jersey. When Conrail was formed in 1976, some of the electric locomotives received the blue color scheme with the white "wheel on a rail" Conrail logo.

Lionel introduced its version of the Virginian rectifier electric in 1958, using a modified GP7 chassis and a foreshortened molded plastic body. Like the New Haven

The Versatile "Virginian Rectifier"
1959 Lionel Catalog, page 22

EP-5, the No. 2329 captured the essence of the prototype, despite the fact that the real locomotive had six wheel trucks and was about the size of a Train Master. Lionel also took some artistic license and used blue as the base carbody color instead of the prototype's black. (This is a similar marketing decision to that made in changing the No. 2331 Virginian Train Master's color to blue in 1956 to make that model more attractive to customers.) The 2329 appeared again in the 1959 catalog, but only to deplete inventory, as sales proved disappointing. Producing a model of a highly distinctive locomotive from a railroad that traversed a sparsely populated area of the country presents certain marketing risks. Consequently, the No. 2329, like a number of briefly produced postwar Lionel diesels, became highly desired by collectors.

Virginian EL-C's 132 and 133 are about one year old in August 1957 as they await their next assignment, which will probably be moving a heavy coal train from Roanoke, Virginia, where they were photographed, to Mullens, West Virginia, the west end of the railroad's electrified trackage. *(Bill Volkmer photo)*

In May 1957 Virginian EL-C's 130 and 131 appear to be newly delivered in Princeton, West Virginia. It's easy to see why these locomotives were nicknamed "bricks" when painted orange on the New Haven RR. *(Don Ball collection)*

STEAM LOCOMOTIVES

MILWAUKEE
HIAWATHA

In 1935, the Chicago, Milwaukee, St. Paul and Pacific Railroad received the first of its Class A "Hiawatha" streamlined passenger locomotives. The graceful orange and gray racehorses represented a revival of the "Atlantic" or 4-4-2 wheel arrangement that was generally superseded over 20 years earlier by heavier passenger power like the "Pacific" or 4-6-2 and even larger machines that evolved later. The limited seating capacity of the self-propelled internal combustion-powered consists like the Burlington's PIONEER ZEPHYR and the Union Pacific's M-10000 as well as the introduction of separate lightweight streamlined passenger cars made the Milwaukee Road consider a steam powered alternative. Collaboration with the American Locomotive Company resulted in the design of a high speed steam locomotive of modest tractive effort (30,700 pounds) equipped with 84 inch drivers and capable of moving a lightweight train at speeds of over 100 mph without difficulty. The first of four of these sleek steel racehorses appeared in 1935; they bore the road numbers 1 through 4. The handsomely styled "Hiawathas" captured the imagi-

nation of the railroad industry and the public with their impressive performance racing across the midwest with a series of new long distance streamlined trains, appropriately named HIAWATHAS.

The attractiveness and fame of the Milwaukee Road's "Hiawatha" locomotives prompted Lionel to produce its version for the Christmas of 1935. Like the M-10000, the highly realistic model was made in full scale size, using 17/64ths of an inch per foot, or 1/45 the size of the prototype. It was designed to operate only on "072" or wider radius track. The most significant departure from the prototype's appearance was the use of two of Lionel's contemporary six wheel sheet metal trucks on the tender. The real locomotive used a six wheel Commonwealth truck at the front of the tender and a four wheel truck at the rear. It was reported that Joshua Lionel Cowan felt that a lack of symmetry caused by dissimilar trucks might detract from the model's sales appeal. Given the impressive marketing skills demonstrated by Mr. Cowan in making his company the leader in toy train production and sales, the choice was probably wise.

The author was fortunate to obtain a 1938 vintage Hiawatha set with its original boxes in 1980. *(William J. Brennan collection)*

Lionel's 250E is a quite accurate replica of the Milwaukee class A, with some allowance for production economics and operation on three rail tubular track. *(William J. Brennan collection)*

The Hiawatha
Top: Remote control streamliner with whistle
Bottom: Remote control freight train with whistle
1937 Lionel Catalog, page 21

The first of the Milwaukee Road's class A "Hiawatha" Atlantic locomotives, No. 1, awaits departure time at the old Milwaukee, Wisconsin station on September 8, 1949. *(Karl Then photo)*

On September 8, 1949, No. 1 departs with a westbound passenger train at Milwaukee, Wisconsin. *(Karl Then photo)*

The Milwaukee Road's pride in its flagship HIAWATHA passenger train fleet is evident from a May 1935 timetable that included a detailed brochure that described the features of the locomotive and cars. *(Robert J. Yanosey collection)*

CHICAGO MILWAUKEE ST. PAUL AND PACIFIC

Hiawatha

AMERICA'S FIRST INTEGRAL STREAMLINED STEAM LOCOMOTIVE AND THE NEWEST TYPE OF STREAM-STYLED SUPER-SPEED TRAIN

Milwaukee also stabled larger Hudson (4-6-4) class steam locomotives streamlined for HIAWATHA service. Hudson 103 is about to depart Milwaukee with a Chicago-bound train. These 84-inch-drivered class F7 locomotives were built by Alco in 1938 and superseded the class A Atlantics. *(Karl Then photo)*

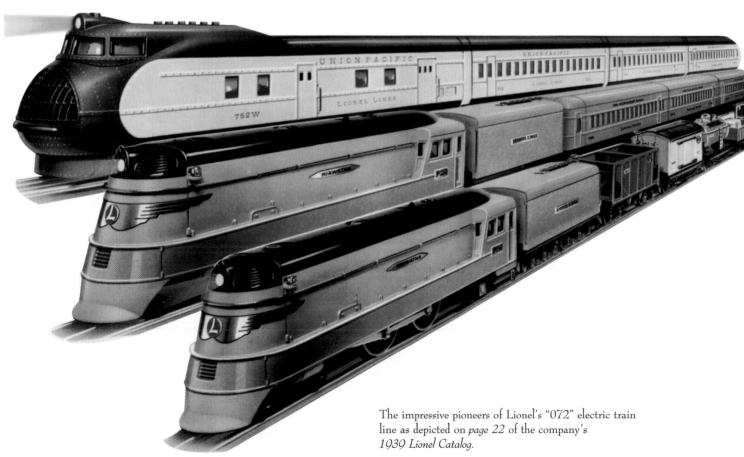

The impressive pioneers of Lionel's "072" electric train line as depicted on *page 22* of the company's *1939 Lionel Catalog.*

THE NEW YORK CENTRAL HUDSON

One of the most famous steam locomotives in the United States and, probably, the world, is the "Hudson" designed for heavy, high speed passenger service on the New York Central Railroad. The first of these beautifully proportioned J-I racehorses that introduced the 4-6-4 wheel arrangement, No. 5200, was christened on St. Valentine's Day of 1927, after pulling out of the erection shop of the American Locomotive Company (Alco). After extensive testing, the 5200 easily met the railroad's expectations, reliably handling heavy trains on surprisingly fast schedules. Consequently, the Central acquired 143 more J-I's over the next four years from Alco, culminating with No. 5344, the last Class J-Ie from Alco in 1931.

No. 5344 would prove to be the most famous "Hudson" of all, partly because it was one of only two American steam locomotives to wear two different streamlined shrouds. It had the distinction of wearing both the COMMODORE VANDERBILT and Henry Dreyfuss-designed TWENTIETH CENTURY LIMITED garb. The other steamer was Baltimore & Ohio's P-7 "Pacific" No. 5304 which was streamlined in 1937 for the ROYAL BLUE and reverted to its conventional appearance in 1940. In 1946, it was refitted with a different streamlined shroud for the CINCINNATIAN.

The fame of No. 5344 was further enhanced in 1937 when Lionel introduced its first 1:48 full scale model locomotive, No. 700E, a nearly exact reproduction of J-Ie "Hudson" No. 5344. After using the 1:45 proportions for the CITY OF PORTLAND and HIAWATHA, the company decided to use the 1/4 inch scale that was sanctioned by the National Model Railroaders Association (NMRA). The result was exquisite; the 700E was the best detailed and most realistic "O" gauge scale model ever mass produced and presents a quite respectable level of realism and detail even to this day. It was reported to be Joshua Lionel Cowan's favorite among all of the model locomotives that his company produced. Zinc alloy pressure die castings provided intricate details such as rivets, metal seams, embossings and journal box covers, while piping, handrails and control linkage were installed as separate parts. It was the first Lionel steam model to feature full working valve gear, even the lubricator linkage. The scale 79" driving wheels were molded with the delicate spokes of the prototype and fine, close-to-scale flanges, unlike the comparatively crude drivers on earlier Lionel locomotives. The only significant omission was the lack of heavier counterweights on the main drivers; the castings for all were identical. The die cast tender, containing a conventional Lionel whistle, even boasted of the same number of rivets (1600) as the prototype. A necessary operating compromise was the installation of a third rail roller pickup at the center of the tender (to power the whistle) where the water scoop would otherwise be located. Most scale model railroads of the era used outside third rails and Lionel included sturdy pickup shoes for this type of operation that the owner could easily install in place of the roller assemblies. Naturally, the 700E found a place on individually owned and club operated scale model railroads across the country and abroad. The $75 price was substantial for the time but was, in fact, lower than the cost of many other contemporary "O" gauge scale model locomotives that were crude by comparison. The 700E, which was manufactured until 1942, is understandably highly prized by collec-

tors of Lionel trains and has been described as the "king" of its "O" gauge line. It was so remarkable that Lionel even introduced a line of solid "T" rail "072" track, crossings and manual and remote control switches to accommodate the scale flanges on the 700E.

In recognition of those customers who operated their trains on tubular "072" track, No. 763, a simplified "Hudson" with much less detail and valve gear and deep flanged wheels

was made available in that same year. A gun-metal version came most frequently with an "oil" tender, the Vanderbilt style offered with the earlier Nos. 255 and 263 locomotives or, quite rarely, a No. 2226W tender with a molded Bakelite coal pile. The black version was accompanied only by the No. 2226W or 2263W, which was similar in proportions to the 700W tender but slightly smaller. This locomotive, too remained in the catalog until 1942.

Mighty Engine of the Century. No. 700 EW Scale Model, Worm-Geared Hudson Locomotive with Built-in Whistle. *1939 Lionel Catalog, page 24*

Classic New York Central J-1 5368 speeds Train 75, THE MERCURY through Dearborn, Michigan in March 1942. Lionel's No. 700E was clearly "on target" as a reproduction of the graceful prototype. *(Emery Gulash photo)*

Unfortunately, these magnificent creations possessed their "Achilles Heel"; many were afflicted with crazing and decomposition of the zinc alloy castings, turning an otherwise extremely valuable collectible into a carcass of value only for its surviving parts. Two theories prevail on the cause of this tragic phenomenon. One is lead contamination; the other is overheating the carefully proportioned mixture of zinc, aluminum and magnesium so that the magnesium burned away. Either occurrence results in an incompatible combination of metals that prevents a stable crystalline structure from forming. Such a casting becomes a "time bomb" as, over the years, the molecular bonds fail and the alloy warps, swells and flakes apart.

On the fiftieth anniversary of both the founding of the company and Joshua Lionel Cowan's marriage, a final version of the full scale "Hudson" appeared in 1950, as a sort of postwar revival of the black No. 763. The new locomotive, No. 773, featured a smoke unit and Magne-Traction, which was introduced in that year. Because magnetically conductive materials were necessary for Magne-Traction to be effective, sintered iron drivers were used with embossed simulated spokes, an esthetic loss as compared with the elegant spoked wheels of the prewar locomotive. The compensating factor was the improved tractive effort, making the No. 773 the most powerful steam locomotive ever produced by Lionel. It was offered with the top-of-the-line passenger and freight train sets in 1950.

The No. 773 returned to the catalog briefly in 1964-66 and was accompanied by a small plastic tender nearly identical to the No. 2046W that usually accompanied significantly smaller postwar locomotives. The 1964 tenders even carried "Pennsylvania" lettering. The combination left much to be desired esthetically and many operators substituted larger tenders such as No. 2426, which accompanied the 1950 version, or reproductions of the 700E tender, which appeared on the market later in response to the demand.

Like the COMMODORE VANDERBILT and the "Torpedo," Lionel produced smaller and lower cost derivatives of the "Hudson" such as Nos. 1666, 224, 225 and 226 before the war and Nos. 726, 736, 646 and 2046 in the postwar period. These brought the familiar New York Central steam locomotive architecture to a wide variety of "O" and "027" passenger and freight train sets.

The graceful lines of the TWENTIETH CENTURY LIMITED streamlined "Hudson" locomotives whose shrouds were designed by Henry Dreyfuss, appeared in 1946 and 1947 in the "027" sized No. 221 2-6-4 locomotive in both passenger and freight train sets. In 1946, the No. 221 was painted gray and the following year in black.

If you find the "family" look of New York Central steam locomotives appealing, reading *NEW YORK CENTRAL Color Photography of Ed Nowak, Volumes 1, 2 and 3*, and *NEW YORK CENTRAL STEAM In Color* will prove to be rewarding. These books were published by Morning Sun Books.

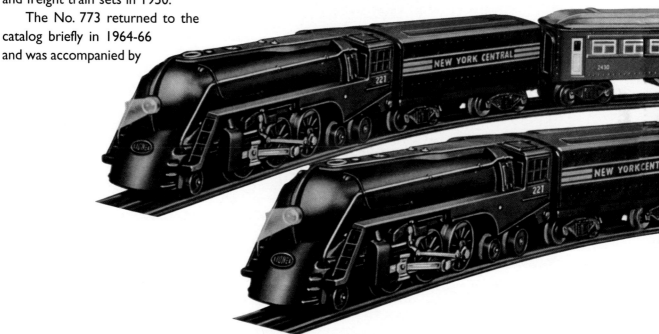

On a clear July 1941 day, Dreyfus-styled streamlined Hudson 5453 leads THE MERCURY through the Detroit, Michigan suburbs toward Chicago. The diminutive Lionel No. 221 reflects the same overall appearance, but reduced considerably from scale size. *(Emery Gulash photo)*

Top: No. 1432 W Lionel Passenger set
Bottom: No. 1433 W Lionel Freight Train
1947 Lionel Catalog, pages 6 & 7

COMMODORE VANDERBILT

In the early 1930's some western roads, particularly the Union Pacific and the Burlington, introduced self-propelled internal combustion powered streamlined lightweight passenger trains. This prompted Carl F. Kantola, an ingenious designer on the staff of the New York Central Railroad to create a streamlined shroud to cover the traditional outline of the last of the company's J-1e "Hudson" passenger locomotives built, No.5344. The locomotive was chosen because the last two J-1's were the only members of the class to be equipped with roller bearings on all axles except for the trailing truck. In the summer of 1934, during the Great Depression, No. 5344 was equipped with the streamlined shrouding that was claimed to reduce air resistance by about 2% and reduce heat losses. One of the railroad's publicity brochures was far more optimistic, claiming a reduction of 35 to 36 per cent. The outline, often described as the "inverted bathtub" was fairly graceful in appearance and nearly disguised the coal-fired, rod-driven nature of the reciprocating machine beneath. The newly-attired 5344 carried the name "Commodore Vanderbilt" and entered revenue service handling the TWENTIETH CENTURY LIMITED between Toledo, Ohio and Chicago on February 19, 1935. The New York Central succeeded in having the best of both worlds, capitalizing on the visual appeal of a graceful streamlined locomotive and retaining the high speed and hauling capacity of its legendary "Hudson" design.

Lionel was sensitive to the appeal of newsworthy developments on the nation's railroads like dramatic new equipment such as streamlined steam locomotives. This prompted the company to produce an "O" gauge version of the "Commodore Vanderbilt" in time for the 1935 holiday season. The model, which was approximately of scale width and height was dramatically shortened to accommodate the 31 inch track circle on which it was designed to operate. Its wheel arrangement was 2-4-2 as compared with the 4-6-4 arrangement on the real "Commodore". The foreshortened tinplate reproduction, however, captured the essence of the prototype and was sufficiently popular to remain in the catalog as No. 264E or No. 265E (a slightly more elaborate model with eccentric rods) with a variety of passenger and freight train sets until 1940. While these locomotives appeared most frequently in the gun metal gray of the prototype, they were also offered in black as well as red and blue to match particular passenger sets like the RED COMET and the BLUE STREAK.

Lionel introduced a slightly smaller version of the "Commodore Vanderbilt" with the same wheel arrangement for compatibility with its "027" freight and passenger train sets, catalog Nos. 289E and 1689E in 1936 and continued production through the following year.

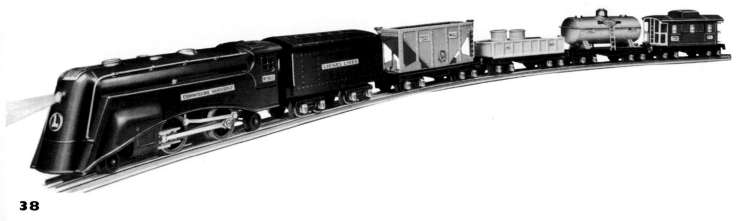

A well-preserved Lionel No. 265 poses for the camera on the layout of its owner, Joel H. Cane.

The "Commodore Vanderbilt"

....World's First Streamlined High Powered Steam Locomotive

NEW YORK CENTRAL LINES

Understandably proud of its graceful streamlining of J-1e, the New York Central published a brochure in 1935 that described the magnificent machine in detail. It even compared the locomotive with the DeWitt Clinton of 1831, the first locomotive to operate in the State of New York. *(Robert J. Yanosey collection)*

THE
PRR
B6

The Pennsylvania Railroad built No. 8026, the first of its class B6 0-6-0's, a heavy six wheel switching locomotive at its Juniata Works in Altoona, Pa. in 1902 for the Lines West (of Pittsburgh). It was a husky, well proportioned machine that became the system's standard heavy switcher and a total of 79 were constructed by Baldwin, Lima and Juniata between 1902 and 1913. The B6, in the opinion of the author, began the familiar "Pennsy" steam locomotive "look" and enjoyed a clean, uncluttered appearance with few outside accessories. Its outside piston valves were actuated by Stephenson link motion which was concealed between the sides of the frames. Later versions featured superheating, (where the steam is heated much higher than the normal boiling point), outside steam delivery pipes from the cylinders, Walschaerts valve gear (outside linkage), and larger fireboxes but were otherwise similar. Superheating was indicated by the addition of a small "s" suffix to the Pennsy road class, so the later modified switchers became class B6s, B6sa, and B6sb.

In 1939, Lionel introduced its first model steam switching locomotive and, possibly, in response to substantial sales of its close to full scale electric trains such as the CITY OF PORTLAND, HIAWATHA and 700E "Hudson", created a quite realistic model of the Pennsylvania's B6 switcher. One version was No. 708, described in the catalog as being built to National Model Railroaders Association (NMRA) standards and compatible with the company's solid "T" rail track

designed for the company's 700E scale model "Hudson" locomotive. Other versions such as the Nos. 227-228 and 230-233 were designed with deeper flanges on their wheels for operation on tubular tinplate track. Options available on these models included an electrically ringing bell in the tender and a direct current-sensitive relay to control either the reverse (Magic Electrol) or the electrically operated (Teledyne) box couplers.

While Lionel's model of the B6 was fairly realistic, it differed slightly from the prototype in that its driving axles were equally spaced, while the real B6's main drivers were closer to the rear pair than the front drivers. When a railroad chose to connect the main rod of a six wheel switcher to the center pair of drivers, the axle was usually located closer to the rear to minimize the angle through which the main rod moved. This was done to reduce the side thrust on the crankpin and crosshead guides and resulting wear. One explanation for this change was Lionel's preference for symmetry and, hopefully, better eye appeal for prospective buyers. In addition, the first B6 had a cab roof whose eaves were relatively straight while Lionel's casting had eaves that tapered upward like the later B6sb. Much discussion has taken place on these minor variances but, in the author's opinion, they do not detract from the overall realism of the models in this series.

As was the case in other locomotive designs, a "lower caste" version was created in 1940 to accommodate conventional tight radius "O" and "O27" gauge track. Shorter

No. 241B
1939 Lionel Catalog, page 21

boiler and tender castings characterized the Nos. 201 and 203 0-6-0's and similar Nos. 1662 and 1663 0-4-0's, versions of which offered selected options such as an electrical bell ringer in the tender or Magic Electrol reversing. Electrically operated box couplers were standard on these locomotives before World War II.

In 1948, the 0-4-0 was reintroduced as No. 1656 with the bell ringing tender and continued until 1949. The box couplers were replaced with coil operated knuckle couplers and the tender featured the new postwar sintered iron truck frames and wheels. From 1955 to 1957, an economy version, No. 1615 appeared with a simplified boiler casting, a plastic tender without bell or light and magnetic trip operated couplers.

Scale Model Pennsylvania B6 Switcher
1939 Lionel Catalog, page 20

Pennsylvania B6sb 5015 posed for the camera in Camden, New Jersey in August 1954.
The locomotive is a later version of the B6 modeled by Lionel with external Walschaerts
valve gear and outside steam delivery pipes to the cylinders. *(Frank C. Kozempel photo)*

These two views of the author's Lionel No. 227 0-6-0 show how, even by contemporary standards, it was extremely realistic and well detailed. The only significant compromise with a full scale appearance was the use of box couplers and deep flanges for compatibility with cars it pulled.

Pennsy's 5015 is at work in Camden, New Jersey in August 1953. The frontal angle shows a closer resemblance to the Lionel 227, 708 and similar switchers. *(Ed Kelsey photo)*

A study of a utilitarian yet handsome switcher at rest, the B6's smaller cousin, the 0-4-0 A5. In this photo, PRR A5 #677 suns itself in 1946 at Aramingo Yard, Philadelphia between assignments. The A5 was particularly useful on the tight radius curves often located right in the cobblestone streets of the Delaware Avenue industrial area. *(Frank Watson photo)*

Lionel's 0-4-0 small steam switcher series is typified by this No.1615. The PRR A5 similarities are most notable in the sloping tender and Belpaire firebox. *(Joel H. Cane collection)*

THE PENNSYLVANIA STEAM TURBINE

As modern steam locomotives increased in size and power, the potential of damage to tracks caused by "dynamic augment" or the forces pounding on the rails because of the massive reciprocating main rods moving up and down at high speeds became greater. The use of the crescent-shaped counterweights that are so familiar on steam locomotive driving wheels, lightweight alloy rods and modern driver designs like the Boxpok and Baldwin Disc helped greatly, but never totally eliminated these forces.

In 1937, the Pennsylvania Railroad began exploring the possibility of replacing the reciprocating machinery of a steam locomotive with a turbine. Sweden experimented with a turbine-powered 2-8-0 freight locomotive in 1932 and, a year later, the British installed a turbine on a 4-6-2 used in high speed passenger service. In both instances, unfortunately, savings in fuel and water consumption were more than offset by increased maintenance costs. The Baldwin Locomotive Works and the Westinghouse Electric Company, manufacturer of many thousands of marine and central power station steam turbines, were confident that they could avoid the problems in the European designs with a higher boiler pressure and lower turbine speeds. The locomo-tive was originally planned to be a 4-8-4, but because it was not constructed until World War II had been well in progress, military priorities made the necessary lightweight alloys unavailable. The increased weight required two additional axles, resulting in a unique 6-8-6 wheel arrangement. No. 6200, with its 6-8-6 wheel arrangement, dwarfed contemporary 4-8-4 Northerns in size and weight, justifying the use of six wheel leading and trailing trucks. For example, the S2 was nearly 40 tons heavier than the Santa Fe's 2900 series 4-8-4's, the heaviest of their wheel arrangement.

In September 1944, Baldwin, in collaboration with Westinghouse, completed experimental S2 No. 6200, the country's first direct-drive steam turbine locomotive at its Eddystone works south of Philadelphia. No. 6200 entered service on October 1, 1944; its turbine's smooth rotational delivery of power eliminated the pounding of conventional pistons and rods by propelling the locomotive through reduction gears. The only rods involved were the side rods connecting the eight driving wheels and these were easy to balance, much like the driving wheels of early electric locomotives. The turbine acquired the nickname "Big Swoosh" because of the lack of the chugging exhaust associated with reciprocating steam power. A retired Pullman conduc-

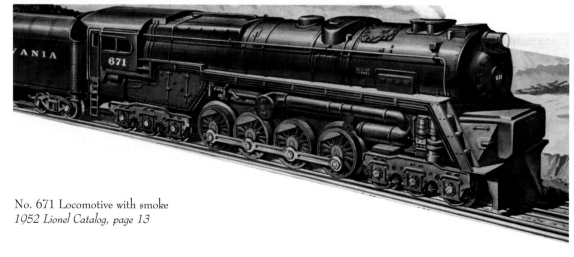

No. 671 Locomotive with smoke
1952 Lionel Catalog, page 13

This Newest Locomotive
is Powered Like a Battleship

LONG AGO successfully developed by Westinghouse for ocean vessels, the *steam turbine* has now been harnessed as a brand-new type of smooth, efficient motive power for modern railroad locomotives.

THE WESTINGHOUSE steam turbine in the Pennsylvania Railroad's new direct-drive locomotive is *no bigger* than a household electric refrigerator—yet it will haul long passenger trains with ease.

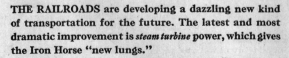

THE POWER-PACKED locomotive turbine is a descendant of giant Westinghouse turbines which generate much of the electricity used today. The great expansion of electric power began with these turbines.

THE RAILROADS are developing a dazzling new kind of transportation for the future. The latest and most dramatic improvement is *steam turbine* power, which gives the Iron Horse "new lungs."

To help produce this new locomotive, the Pennsylvania Railroad, a long-time pioneer in transportation improvements, turned to Westinghouse and the Baldwin Locomotive Works. Working as a team, these companies have produced this latest in a great line of

THE VELVETY FLOW of power from this 6,900 horsepower *steam turbine* locomotive will make trains run with extra smoothness and is a major contribution to finer transportation for the future.

steam locomotives—descended from "Old Ironsides," built by Matthias Baldwin in 1832. *Westinghouse Electric & Manufacturing Company, Pittsburgh 30, Pennsylvania.*

Westinghouse
PLANTS IN 25 CITIES · OFFICES EVERYWHERE

Westinghouse presents: JOHN CHARLES THOMAS—*Sunday 2:30 pm, EWT, NBC*

MARCH 1945 · SCIENTIFIC AMERICAN 147

The Pennsylvania S2 steam turbine locomotive was regarded as such a technological advancement that Westinghouse saw fit to advertise it in the March 1945 issue of *Scientific American*. (William J. Brennan collection)

tor reported his experiences in his only ride behind No. 6200, first noticing the smooth acceleration resembling that of a GG1 electric locomotive and later concluding what proved to be his fastest run from Harrisburg to Altoona, Pennsylvania. The S2 could easily reach 100 mph with a heavy passenger train exceeding 900 tons. While it was quite efficient at high speeds, its consumption of coal and water at low speeds greatly exceeded that of reciprocating steam locomotives of similar size.

However promising this machine seemed to be when it was new, its maintenance history left much to be desired. Between October 1, 1944 and March 13, 1947, No. 6200 was out of service 54% of the time. Failures of firebox staybolts and, to a lesser extent, seals and turbine blades finally led to its withdrawal from service on or about July 14, 1949, as diesel-electric locomotives clearly offered more reliable and economical operation. The Pennsy accepted the inevitable and the S2 was finally scrapped at Conway, Pennsylvania, near Pittsburgh on June 29, 1952. One can speculate that modern space-age materials and drastically increasing oil prices might once again render a coal-fired steam locomotive like the 6200 economically viable.

For Lionel collectors, the Pennsylvania's steam turbine lives on in miniature likenesses

that were some of the company's best known steam locomotives, being produced in several variations from 1946 to 1955. In deference to the sharp curves these tinplate creations were expected to negotiate, they were far smaller than a 1/4 inch scale model would be. The skilled design and production staff at the Irvington/Hillside factory managed to keep the essence of the prototype's rugged appearance in a powerful, smooth running die-cast model. From 1946 to 1949, No. 671 featured die-cast driving wheels with nickel rims. Like many other model steam locomotive in the company's "027" and "O" gauge electric train line, the turbine appeared with Magne-Traction and sintered iron drivers in 1950 and acquired the number 681.

In 1954-55 a final version of the turbine appeared with lubricator linkage on the first driving axle and a narrow white stripe on each running board, as No. 682, the most desirable collectible of these postwar steamers.

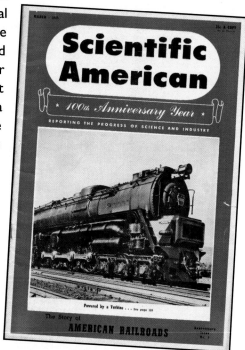

The S2 turbine, No. 6200 was considered so significant by *Scientific American* that it appeared on the magazine's front cover in March 1945.
(William J. Brennan collection)

The S2 posed for a publicity photo on the PRR's famous Horseshoe Curve west of Altoona in late 1944. While the diesel had already proved its worth on other railroads, the Pennsy was determined to create a fleet of "modern" steam locomotives. Known for its exhaustive testing and development of new locomotives, a lot rode on the success of #6200. (PRR photo)

The 2020 was the 0-27 version of the 671 first offered in 1946 less than two years after the "real" #6200 hit the rails. (Joel H. Cane collection)

No. 671 Locomotive with smoke
1952 Lionel Catalog, page 14 and 15

SANTA FE
HUDSON

I n 1937, the Baldwin Locomotive Works constructed five 4-6-4 "Hudson" steam locomotives for heavy, fast passenger service on the Santa Fe Railroad; they became known as the 3460 Class. They boasted of 49,300 pounds of tractive effort and were among the heaviest locomotives of that wheel arrangement. One of these 84" drivered greyhounds was streamlined in an attractive light blue shroud and acquired the nickname "The Blue Goose". The 3460's shared the distinctive modern Santa Fe steam locomotive architecture with contemporary 4-8-4 "Northerns" and 2-10-4 "Texas" types and were similarly recognized for excellence in performance and lasted into the mid-1950's.

The graceful, yet rugged lines of the 3460's inspired Lionel to produce its version of the Santa Fe speedster in 1954. Entirely new dies were made for the locomotive and tender, which were well proportioned and detailed and captured the essence of the prototype. The company assigned the numbers 665 for inclusion in "O" Gauge sets and 2065 for "027". A full 1/4 inch scale model would have been considerably larger than the 700E or 773 and dwarfed most of the cars that the company was marketing at the time, so the model was "downsized" for compatibility and is often described by collectors of Lionel trains as the "small Hudson" to differentiate it from the slightly larger, New York Central-inspired Nos. 646 and 2046. The 2065 was produced until 1956; the 665 continued until 1958 and reappeared for one year in 1966.

Photographs of the various classes of modern Santa Fe steam locomotives in action appear in the four volumes on this railroad (*Santa Fe 1940-1971 In Color*) published by Morning Sun Books.

Santa Fe 2928 and 2921 pose at the Wellington, Kansas division point in April 1955.
They share the front end architecture of Lionel's 665 and 2065 "Small Hudson" models,
even though the prototypes are 4-8-4's. *(L.E. Stagner photo)*

Lionel's Mightiest "027" Steam Locomotive! No. 2065
with smoke, whistle, magne-traction!
1956 Lionel Catalog, page 12

An opportunity missed! The Blue Goose #3460 was the glamour
girl of the Santa Fe steam fleet but Lionel didn't choose to copy
her. Here the 4-6-4 is serviced at Kansas City, KS on July 11,
1953 in the company of a Baldwin switcher.
(Harold Henri, Lou Schmitz collection)

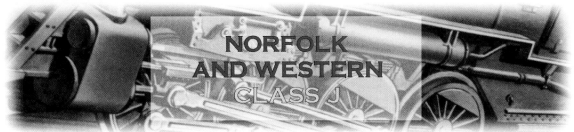

NORFOLK
AND WESTERN
CLASS J

A select few of America's railroad companies were capable of constructing large numbers of their locomotive fleets. The best known among this elite group was the Pennsylvania Railroad with its massive, world-famous Altoona Works in Pennsylvania. The modest-sized Norfolk and Western Railway, a Pennsylvania affiliate, was capable of not only building its own steam locomotives but of creating innovative designs and, consequently, superbly performing high speed passenger power, fast freight haulers and luggers capable of efficiently moving mile-long coal drags across the Blue Ridge Mountains. The road's principal passenger route ran from Norfolk, Virginia near where the James River enters Chesapeake Bay, to Cincinnati, Ohio and the N&W found it necessary to handle increasingly heavy trains over mountain grades at competitively fast schedules.

In 1941, with the clouds of war involvement on the horizon, the first of a series of streamlined 4-8-4 "Northerns" emerged from the Roanoke, Virginia construction shop of the Norfolk and Western Railway. No. 600, the first of the railroad's Class J though gracefully streamlined, was the most powerful locomotive of its wheel arrangement, boasting of over 80,000 pounds of tractive effort. This machine, despite its small (for passenger power) 70 inch driving wheels and stout boiler, presented a sufficiently graceful appearance to be a serious contender as the most attractive streamlined steam locomotive in America. Fourteen of these splendid performers entered service over the ensuing years, completing the series when No. 613 left the erecting hall at Shaffers Crossing in Roanoke in 1950. In 1946, the railroad introduced the streamlined Pullman-built POWHATAN ARROW, Trains 25 and 26 which connected Norfolk and Cincinnati. The train was considered to be comparable to the DAYLIGHTS of the Southern Pacific or the TWENTIETH CENTURY LIMITED of the New York Central. One wonders if the selection of train numbers, the same as the CENTURY was a coincidence. By 1960, these sleek steel racehorses were sidelined and all were scrapped except No. 611, which was preserved as an example of its class. In the 1980's, it was restored to active excursion service and demonstrated its impressive performance to new generations. The company's capable designers created steam locomotives that performed so well that the first post-World War II diesels did not offer the relative operating economies that would justify their purchase. The N&W was therefore the last class I railroad to operate a large roster of modern steam power that did not succumb to the diesels until the late 1950's and became a mecca for railroad historians of that period.

At a very late stage in the operations of steam locomotives by major railroads in this country, Lionel introduced its ingeniously designed model of the Norfolk and Western Railway Class J. The model was reported to be inspired by an employee of the railroad who modified a No. 736 "Berkshire" 2-8-4 into a fairly realistic model of the streamliner and sent photographs of it to Lionel's offices. The idea apparently appealed to the company's marketing staff and No. 746 made its appearance in 1957 and it remained in the catalog until 1960. The No. 746 was considerably smaller than a scale model Class J, but it was well-proportioned and captured the effect of the prototype. In deference to production economics, its drive mechanism was very similar to the No. 736 "Berkshire". A plastic tender nearly identical to the No. 2046W accompanied the J, which was offered only with freight trains, without regard to the passenger duties performed by the real locomotives. Nonetheless, the No. 746 has become a highly regarded collectible among collectors of Lionel's postwar trains.

Norfolk and Western's 604 rolls the twelve cars of Train 15, THE CAVALIER through Ripplemead, Virginia in May 1958. The resemblance to Lionel's No. 746 is striking despite the reduction from scale size to accommodate the sharp tinplate curves. *(Robert Malinoski photo)*

No. 746 LTS Norfolk and Western
Steam Locomotive and Whistle Tender
1959 Lionel Catalog, page 36

A picture of speed and power! Freshly-washed #605 with its proud engineer at the throttle poses at Bristol, VA on July 5, 1957. Lionel certainly captured the essence of this mighty locomotive. *(J.J. Buckley photo)*

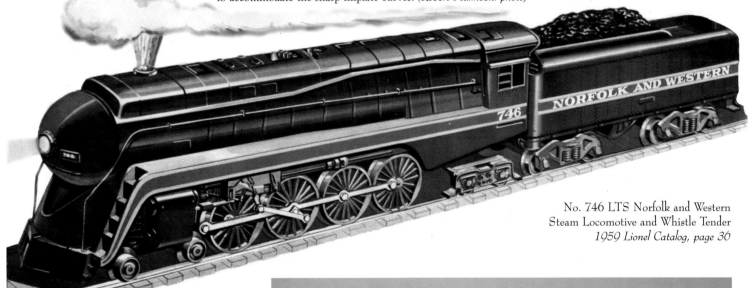

CHEVROLET OK USED CARS AND TRUCKS

Change-um oil filter... car run heap better" PurOlator

From the earliest "teakettles on wheels" ...from the hand-stoked woodburners with their high stacks...from the brawny Moguls, Hudsons and Consolidateds that fought two World Wars...comes this

MAGNIFICENT HEIR ON SUPER "O" TRA

No. 3356

LIONEL 6557

NEW! No. 6557

No. 746LTS

NORFOLK AND WESTERN 746

OUTFIT No. 2525WS

AVAILABLE FOR SEPARATE SALE

For items not described, see index page 45.

No. 746LTS Norfolk & Western Steam Loco and Whistle Tender—Proof that steam can be modern and efficient! Equipped with Magne-Traction; super-beam headlight and illuminated marker lights; Lionel steam-type whistle; and a cool-running smoke generator using smoke fluid for safe smoke-puffing hours on end. Loco and tender 21½" long. $49.95

NEW! No. 6557 Smoking Caboose—A new Lionel "first"! This illuminated caboose carries an operating smoke generator that streams real smoke. No. 909 Smoke Fluid included. Caboose 7" long. $6.95

No. 3356 Operating Horse Car—H actually come out of car by remote contr go down ramp, move around water troug proceed back up the other ramp and into Open corral gate and horses herd to the w ing trough. Car, horses, ramps, corral incl Car 11¼" long, corral 10½" x 6".

Norfolk and Western 611 rolls what appears to be the POWHATAN ARROW through Christiansburg, Virginia on July 3, 1957. *(J.J. Buckley photo)*

Class J 609 approaches the platform at Abingdon, Virginia on August 30, 1957. *(J.J. Buckley photo)*

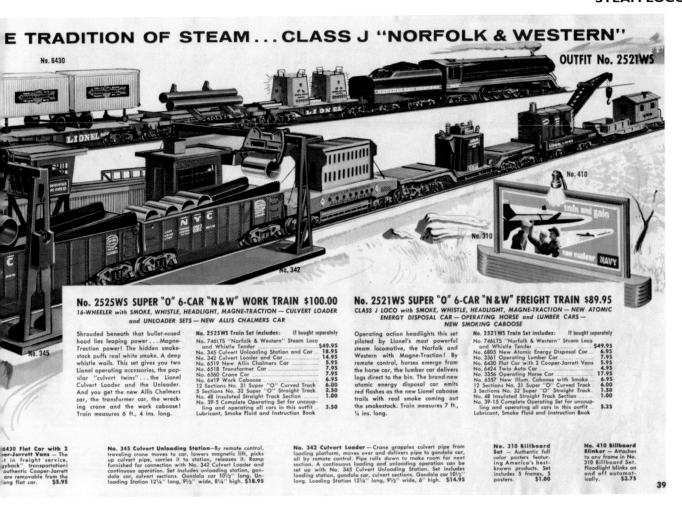

E TRADITION OF STEAM...CLASS J "NORFOLK & WESTERN"

No. 6430

OUTFIT No. 2521WS

No. 342

No. 345

No. 410

No. 310

train and gain

raw nuclear

NAVY

No. 2525WS SUPER "O" 6-CAR "N&W" WORK TRAIN $100.00
16-WHEELER with SMOKE, WHISTLE, HEADLIGHT, MAGNE-TRACTION — CULVERT LOADER and UNLOADER SETS — NEW ALLIS CHALMERS CAR

Shrouded beneath that bullet-nosed hood lies leaping power...Magne-Traction power! The hidden smoke-stack puffs real white smoke. A deep whistle wails. This set gives you two Lionel operating accessories, the popular "culvert twins"...the Lionel Culvert Loader and the Unloader. And you get the new Allis Chalmers car, the transformer car, the wrecking crane and the work caboose! Train measures 6 ft., 4 ins. long.

No. 2525WS Train Set includes:	If bought separately
No. 746LTS "Norfolk & Western" Steam Loco and Whistle Tender	$49.95
No. 345 Culvert Unloading Station and Car	18.95
No. 342 Culvert Loader and Car	14.95
No. 6519 New Allis Chalmers Car	5.95
No. 6518 Transformer Car	7.95
No. 6560 Crane Car	7.95
No. 6419 Work Caboose	6.95
12 Sections No. 31 Super "O" Curved Track	6.00
5 Sections No. 32 Super "O" Straight Track	2.50
No. 48 Insulated Straight Track Section	1.00
No. 39-5 Complete Operating Set for uncoupling and operating all cars in this outfit	3.50
Lubricant, Smoke Fluid and Instruction Book	

No. 2521WS SUPER "O" 6-CAR "N&W" FREIGHT TRAIN $89.95
CLASS J LOCO with SMOKE, WHISTLE, HEADLIGHT, MAGNE-TRACTION — NEW ATOMIC ENERGY DISPOSAL CAR — OPERATING HORSE and LUMBER CARS — NEW SMOKING CABOOSE

Operating action headlights this set piloted by Lionel's most powerful steam locomotive, the Norfolk and Western with Magne-Traction! By remote control, horses emerge from the horse car, the lumber car delivers logs direct to the bin. The brand-new atomic energy disposal car emits red flashes as the new Lionel caboose trails with real smoke coming out the smokestack. Train measures 7 ft., ¼ ins. long.

No. 2521WS Train Set includes:	If bought separately
No. 746LTS "Norfolk & Western" Steam Loco and Whistle Tender	$49.95
No. 6805 New Atomic Energy Disposal Car	6.95
No. 3361 Operating Lumber Car	7.95
No. 6430 Flat Car with 2 Cooper-Jarrett Vans	5.95
No. 6424 Twin Auto Car	4.95
No. 3356 Operating Horse Car	17.95
No. 6557 New Illum. Caboose with Smoke	6.95
12 Sections No. 31 Super "O" Curved Track	6.00
3 Sections No. 32 Super "O" Straight Track	1.50
No. 48 Insulated Straight Track Section	1.00
No. 39-15 Complete Operating Set for uncoupling and operating all cars in this outfit	5.25
Lubricant, Smoke Fluid and Instruction Book	

6430 Flat Car with 2 -per-Jarrett Vans — The st in freight service, gyback" transportation! authentic Cooper-Jarrett are removable from the ong flat car. **$5.95**

No. 345 Culvert Unloading Station—By remote control, traveling crane moves to car, lowers magnetic lift, picks up culvert pipe, carries it to station, releases it. Ramp furnished for connection with No. 342 Culvert Loader and continuous operation. Set includes unloading station, gondola car, culvert sections. Gondola car 10½" long. Unloading Station 12¼" long, 9½" wide, 8¼" high. **$18.95**

No. 342 Culvert Loader — Crane grapples culvert pipe from loading platform, moves over and delivers pipe to gondola car, all by remote control. Pipe rolls down to make room for next section. A continuous loading and unloading operation can be set up with No. 345 Culvert Unloading Station. Set includes loading station, gondola car, culvert sections. Gondola car 10½" long. Loading Station 12¼" long, 9½" wide, 6" high. **$14.95**

No. 310 Billboard Set — Authentic full color posters featuring America's best-known products. Set includes 5 frames, 5 posters. **$1.00**

No. 410 Billboard Blinker — Attaches to any frame in No. 310 Billboard Set. Floodlight blinks on and off automatically. **$2.75**

39

Norfolk and Western also streamlined a number of its Class K2 (4-8-2) Mountain types to resemble the Class J's. No. 130 awaits servicing at Shenandoah, Virginia. (*Frank Watson photo*)

ARTICULATED DIESEL STREAMLINERS

THE
FLYING
YANKEE

In the spring of 1934, the Chicago, Burlington & Quincy Railroad introduced its PIONEER ZEPHYR, a stainless steel three-car articulated streamlined train. The Zephyr was constructed by the Budd Company of Philadelphia using a new technique of spot welding stainless steel and powered by an eight cylinder 600 hp Winton diesel engine supplied by General Motors. The train, which represented a drastic technological change from the conventional passenger trains of the time, impressed the Boston & Maine and Maine Central sufficiently to order a very similar consist which was named the FLYING YANKEE, entering service in 1935. These trains successfully demonstrated the reliability, economy and performance of Diesel-electric power but were limited by the seating capacity of a three or four car consist. The future would see diesel locomotives grow in size and power to the extent that they could replace the most powerful steam passenger locomotives handling heavy trains of conventional rolling stock.

Lionel introduced its "O" gauge version of the FLYING YANKEE in 1935 and continued to manufacture several variations until 1941. To accommodate the sharp curves around which the train was designed to operate, the model was significantly reduced in length and the cross section was slightly smaller than full 1/4 inch scale. The stainless steel exterior of the prototype was simulated by chrome plating the sheet metal bodies on most versions and applying satin finished silver paint on others. The power car roof and drive wheels were made of die cast zinc alloy and the train was powered by a "plate" motor technologically similar to the company's steam locomotives' motors of the period. A direct current controlled whistle similar to that used on the company's steam locomotives was offered on most of the sets. The chrome plated four car set with gunmetal nose and observation end with a whistle is the most common, with the all chrome and satin finished versions being rarer and more attractive to collectors.

Boston & Maine's FLYING YANKEE leaves Greenfield, Massachusetts headed for Boston in July 1954. *(Ed Kelsey photo)*

After over 20 years of service, the FLYING YANKEE was preserved at the Edaville Railroad at South Carver, Massachusetts and was photographed in June 1966. *(William J. Brennan photos)*

"Pilot" Daniels, they call him, and he's dean of B. and M. enginemen on the Yankee.

The FLYING YANKEE

Streamlined and sheathed in an armor of gleaming steel, the famous Flying Yankee, pride of the Boston and Maine Railroad, whips along the rails between the bay city and Portland in a new, express service of streaking speed.

No. 267E "O" Gauge Distant Control Flying Yankee Streamliner

Outfit consists of:
1— No. 616E Distant Control power car
2— No. 617 Coaches
1— No. 618 Observation car
1— No. 88 Reversing controller
8— OC curved, 4— OS straight track
1— OTC Lockon

Replica of the Boston and Maine's famous Flying Yankee. Built of steel and richly embellished by a wealth of accurate detail. Fluted in the characteristic fashion of the streamliner. Finished in a highly polished chromium plate that permanently resists tarnish, dullness and corrosion. The motor compartment of the power car and the rear of the observation car are finished in a harmonizing gun metal. Cars are ingeniously coupled by means of vestibules which contain lights for interior illumination. Equipped with a powerful, high-efficiency motor that swivels, with the turning of the train, in a ball and socket joint. Train is 42 inches long. Track supplied forms an oval 50 by 30 inches.   Price $10.95

Type "B" Lionel Multivolt transformer will operate this t... greater capacity, will provi...

Enclosed lounge and observation platform.

Cars couple into ingenious vestibules that contain four-wheel swivel trucks.

Chisel-shaped prow with wide-range windows, louvers and exhaust stacks.

The B&M FLYING YANKEE and CB&Q PIONEER ZEPHYR were the "final word" in modern passenger train travel in the late 1930's.

the PIONEER Zephyr

America's First Diesel-Powered Streamlined Train...

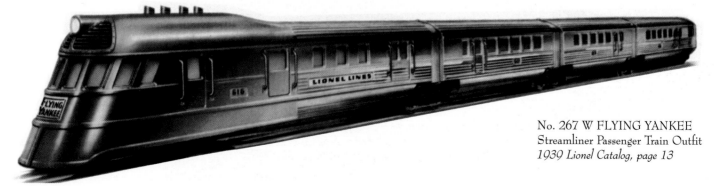

No. 267 W FLYING YANKEE
Streamliner Passenger Train Outfit
1939 Lionel Catalog, page 13

By 1944 the FLYING YANKEE's 142-passenger capacity was insufficient to meet wartime demands on the Bangor, Maine to Boston run, so the 6000 was reassigned to the White River Junction-Boston CHESHIRE. Seen at Waverly in 1945 the serviceman at right would soon return home and witness some of Lionel's most productive years. *(Donald S. Robinson photo)*

Proudly proclaiming CHESHIRE on its nose, the 6000 wyes itself at Bellows Falls, VT in 1950. The ball signal was an antique even at this time. *(Donald S. Robinson photo)*

Burlington's MARK TWAIN ZEPHYR, a near look-alike to the FLYING YANKEE awaits its next departure at Burlington, Iowa in the early 1950's. *(Jim Ewinger photo)*

The first successful stainless steel diesel powered streamliner, the PIONEER ZEPHYR pauses under the St. Joseph Union Station trainshed in December 1957. The train would finally be preserved at Chicago's Museum of Science and Industry. *(Richard A. Wolter photo)*

The Burlington was extremely proud of its advancements in pasenger train modernization and issued this colorful booklet to the public. *(R.J. Yanosey collection)*

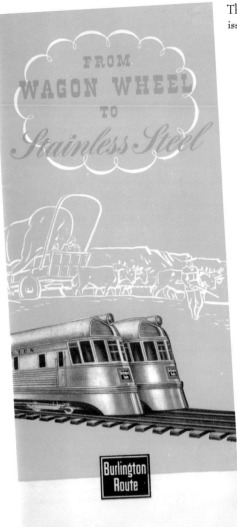

Burlington ZEPHYR 9902 loads passengers at Hannibal, Missouri for an eastbound trip to Chicago. *(Mike Gleason photo)*

The MARK TWAIN ZEPHYR pauses at the Keokuk, Iowa in July 1949. The train followed the Mississippi River from St. Louis to Burlington, Iowa, inspiring the pen name of Samuel Clemens, who piloted riverboats on that waterway. *(Charles Franzen photo)*

UNION PACIFIC
M-1000
STREAMLINER

In February 1934, at the Pullman-Standard plant near Chicago, the Union Pacific Railroad exhibited an experimental aluminum alloy train called the M-10000, also known as the CITY OF SALINA, a three car articulated streamliner. The articulation and the use of full width vestibules between the cars gave the impression of a single seamless carbody. The aluminum alloy used, Duraluminum, was reported to as strong as steel at one-third the weight, so that the three car train weighed about the same as a single heavyweight steel passenger car. A spark ignition engine with twelve 7.5 by 8.5 inch cylinders was fueled by distillate, a petroleum product that is slightly heavier and less volatile (and less explosive) than gasoline. The train's styling was novel, with a turret cab atop a bulbous nose with a large air intake on the power car that observers of the time described as an enlarged earthworm and inward sloping car sides that suggested an "egg-shaped" cross section on the carbodies. The train was operat-

ed on a 12,000 mile tour that covered 65 cities and included a personal inspection by President Franklin D. Roosevelt in Washington, D.C. Along with the Burlington's PIONEER ZEPHYR and the Boston & Maine's FLYING YANKEE, the train introduced the concept of high speed lightweight, limited seating capacity trains powered by internal combustion engines, distillate or diesel. The success of the M-10000 prompted the Union Pacific to build other similar trains, including the M-10001, or CITY OF PORTLAND, a six car train with considerably different locomotive and car configurations from those on the pioneer unit. The train entered regular service in 1935, powered with a 900 hp 201-A 12cylinder diesel engine to handle the longer consist.

Lionel introduced a very realistic model of the M-10000 in 1934, using heavy gauge sheet metal sides and roofs and zinc alloy die cast noses, floors and ends that were its state-of-the-art in model train manufacturing of that era. The power and trailing cars carried the catalog numbers 752, 753 and 754 and Lionel chose to name it the CITY OF PORTLAND, apparently preferring to use the name of a more prominent city to describe its new streamliner. The most significant departure from prototype appearance was the use of an inboard design on the power and "vestibule" trucks where the wheels were exposed, unlike the real consist's streamliner trucks with outside frames. It was powered by a smooth running plate motor of a design similar to that used on the company's model steam locomotives. The power car with a D.C. controlled whistle identical to that used on contemporary steam types was offered as an option on the 752W. Lionel produced the train in the prototypical colors of brown and yellow until 1941 as well as a solid satin silver scheme until 1936. From 1936 to 1941, a four car set was available with the addition of a 753 coach. All versions are highly prized collectibles among model train hobbyists.

This is a good point to mention the compromise involving the sizing of most "O" gauge scale model trains, which have been designed to be 1/48 the size of their prototypes. The track gauge, however is 1 1/4 inches, which is the equivalent of a five-foot gauge, rather than the four foot, eight and one-half inches used by American railroads. The discrepancy is minor, but caused some purists to build models based on 17/64 of an inch to the foot (1:45) to render the superstructures to be in exact proportion to the track gauge of 1 1/4 inches. Lionel used this scale in producing its Union Pacific M-10000 in 1934 and Milwaukee Road "Hiawatha" streamlined Atlantic in the following year. When the company introduced the 700EW full scale model Hudson in 1937, it returned to the more commonly used scale of 1:48 and retained it for its subsequent models intended to be "O" gauge "scale" size.

The evolution of the diesel powered streamlined passenger train continued as separate, free standing powered units described as models TA and TB appeared. The Union

Pacific purchased six such units in 1936 from Pullman-Standard in 1936 to handle the two consists of its new streamliner, the CITY OF DENVER. Each unit rode on a pair of powered four wheel trucks equipped with D.C. traction motors and was propelled by a 1200 hp V-16 Winton diesel from General Motors. The next steps in this progression would be the production E2 and later E-series passenger locomotives that GM's Electro-Motive Division would pour out of LaGrange to begin the wholesale replacement of steam power in this service.

In the same year, Lionel introduced its version of the CITY OF DENVER with understandable artistic license in deference to production economics as well as its tightly curved "O" gauge tinplate trackage. The prototype TA units were comparable in size to the postwar F3's, so full scale models would have required a series of larger passenger cars. Depression era economics probably precluded another "072" streamliner like the No. 752. No. 636 consequently appeared in a reduction from full scale size and shared the configuration with the No. 616 FLYING YANKEE of the preceding year, with the sheet metal articulated cars painted in the brown and yellow color scheme of the prototype. Technology was advancing, however and the power car body shell was a single zinc alloy die casting instead of the sheet metal fabrication of the No. 616. This would become the production technique of choice for Lionel's future steam locomotives and, after the war, the GG1 electric. To the customers of the period as well as the collectors of subsequent decades, Lionel's creation still captured the essence of the real streamliner that conveyed passengers between Chicago and the Rockies.

The author's CITY OF PORTLAND.

In a Union Pacific publicity photo, the nearly new CITY OF DENVER poses a few miles east of its namesake city with the Rocky Mountains in the background. Ownership was shared with the Chicago & North Western which operated the train from Chicago to the Union Pacific at Council Bluffs, IA. *(UP RR museum- KS42)*

The
LIONEL
Union Pacific
"CITY OF DENVER"

No. 299W "O" GAUGE STREAMLINER WITH WHISTLE

Outfit consists of:
1— No. 636W Distant Control power car   1— No. 66 Whistle and reversing controller
2— No. 637 Illuminated Coaches   8— OC curved, 4— OS straight track
1— No. 638 Illuminated Observation car   1— OTC Lockon

Authentic model of the Union Pacific Railroad's new "City of Denver" that races at a top clip from Chicago to the Colorado City. Sister-streamliner to the famous brown and yellow U. P. "City of Portland" that dazzled the nation and won the heart of every boy with its record-breaking trans-continental speeds.

This thrilling Lionel model is equipped with a real railroad whistle and remote control. The motor has double-reduction gears for hauling heavy trains without lowering its pace. Cars are coupled into vestibules containing the wheels and lights for interior illumination. A button on the top of each vestibule is pressed to couple and uncouple cars. The power car is a castings containing all of the minute details of the real trains. Radiator front is a modern design A chromium plated duplicate of the real railroad emblem adorns the side of the motor car. Train is finished in rich golden brown and yellow enamel, fluted to accentuate its lustre. Train is 42½ inches long. Track supplied forms an oval 50 by 30 inches. Price $15.75

Type "B" Lionel Multi-volt transformer will operate this train. Type "T" transformer, of greater capacity, will provide for the addition of many illuminated and automatic accessories.

14

LIONEL *Union Pacific* CITY OF DENVER

● **No. 299W "O" GAUGE REMOTE CONTROL STREAMLINE OUTFIT WITH WHISTLE**

Authentic model of the Union Pacific Railroad's new "City of Denver" that races at a top clip out of Chicago twice a week. Sister-streamliner to the famous U. P. "City of Portland" that dazzled the nation and won the heart of every boy with its record-breaking trans-continental speeds. Outfit consists of: No. 636W Distant Control power car, two No. 637 Illuminated coaches, No. 638 Illuminated Observation car, No. 66 Whistle and reversing controller, eight sections of OC curved track, four sections of OS straight track and Lockon. Train measures 42½ inches. Track forms an oval 50 by 30 inches. **Price $16.50**

This thrilling Lionel model is equipped with the Lionel railroad whistle that is built into the power car. You can sit at any distance from the track and, by merely pressing a button, make the train sound any railroad whistle. Remote control reversing is also a built-in feature. The motor in the power car has double-reduction gears for hauling heavy trains without lowering its fast pace. Cars are coupled into vestibules containing the wheels and lights for interior illumination. A button on the top of each vestibule is pressed to couple and uncouple the cars.

No. 636W. Power car with whistle and controller.   Price $10.00
No. 637. Coach with one vestibule.   Price $3.75

Type "B" Lionel Transformer will operate this train. Type "T", will provide for the addition of many accessories.

The sixteen cylinder Winton engines are revving up as the CITY OF DENVER departs the Chicago & North Western station in the Windy City in August 1948. *(Dick Townley photo)*

POSTWAR DIESEL LOCOMOTIVES

THE ELECTRO-MOTIVE F3

After World War II, our country's railroads swiftly embraced the more economical Diesel locomotives as replacements for the labor-intensive steam powered "Iron Horses" that served the industry for well over a century. A wide variety of attractively styled road diesels like the elegant EMD E6 or E7 or the Alco PA-1 might have been promising subjects for Lionel to reproduce in "O" gauge but, unless these units were drastically foreshortened, the models could not operate around the 31 inch circle of the company's tinplate track. The shorter four axle freight or dual service units would better lend themselves to Lionel's practical operating limitations. As events unfolded, the choice among these was made by discussions with and later contributions by interested parties.

The introduction of the Lionel "O" gauge model of the Electro-Motive Division of General Motors (EMD) 1500 h.p. dual service F3 cab unit in 1948 brought the toy train manufacturer into the postwar diesel era. While the company had previously produced models of the prewar articulated streamliners, the F3 was the first true road diesel locomotive in its line. According to reliable sources, three quarters of the cost of the tooling was shared equally by the EMD division of General Motors, the New York Central Railroad and the Santa Fe Railroad. The result was a near-scale model of a Phase III F3 which was then still in production at EMD's plant in La Grange, Illinois. The Phase III was the third body style used on this type of locomotive and is characterized by having low, conical radiator fan shrouds on the roof and two portholes and a series of four louvres on each side. Until 1952, the Lionel F3 would appear only in Santa Fe and New York Central liveries, reportedly as part of the agreement that funded the tooling for the unit. Also, at the bottom of the rear door of each cab unit a small rectangle with the letters "GM" appeared.

*Front Cover
1952 Lionel Catalog*

IT HAPPENS 150 TIMES A DAY IN CHICAGO

A MEASURE of the railroads' high preference for General Motors Diesel locomotives can be found in Chicago, hub of the nation's railways.

There, high-speed mainline passenger trains arrive or depart behind a General Motors Diesel 150 times every day.

Similarly an array of General Motors Diesel-powered trains arrives and departs every day at Washington, Denver, Kansas City, St. Louis, New Orleans, Seattle, Miami, Atlanta, Los Angeles, Minneapolis-St. Paul, Jacksonville, Omaha — in fact at almost every large railroad terminal in the country.

These General Motors Diesel-powered trains include more than 150 of America's most famous "name" trains — the fast flyers and streamliners that have so

greatly increased railway travel.

Such overwhelming endorsement by leading railroads is based on operating experience covering more than one and one-half billion passenger train car-miles piled up behind these locomotives since General Motors pioneered the Diesel mainline locomotives in 1934.

This experience has demonstrated that General Motors Diesels maintain faster, more regular "on time" schedules, cost less to operate, require less maintenance and service and have a far longer useful life than any other type of locomotive.

All of which explains why General Motors is now the world's largest builder of locomotives, and why smart travelers say "the best trains follow General Motors locomotives!"

ELECTRO-MOTIVE DIVISION
GENERAL MOTORS · LA GRANGE, ILL.
Home of the Diesel locomotive

GM GENERAL MOTORS LOCOMOTIVES

General Motors visibly showed off its cab units in its advertisements of the late 1940's. *(R.J. Yanosey collection)*

From a collector's point of view, it is fortunate that the author's Lionel No. 2353 was not extensively operated and played with by youngsters, so its silver paint remains pristine. *(Wm. J. Brennan photo)*

Santa Fe 326 awaits its next assignment in Chicago, Illinois on March 1, 1966. The unit is an Electro-Motive F7, a slightly newer diesel cab unit than the F3 modeled by Lionel, but the paint schemes were identical. *(Karl C. Henkels photo, R.J. Yanosey collection)*

The units carried a catalog number of 2333, regardless of whether they wore the Santa Fe's colorful red and silver "Warbonnet" or the New York Central's dignified two tone gray "lightning stripe" color scheme, and were sold in pairs with one unit powered by two motors and the other unpowered. The engine was equipped with a bicycle buzzer horn activated by a size "D" flashlight battery and a conventional Lionel direct current triggered whistle/horn relay. At the time, the F3 was the most powerful locomotive in the Lionel line and, like the rest of the company's trains, was of solid construction and ran reliably. The combination of spur and worm gears that transmitted power from the horizontally mounted motors to the wheels, caused a low pitched growl as the model was running and strongly resembled the sound of the prototype.

The real F3 was powered by a 16 cylinder two-cycle 567 series diesel engine that drove a main generator to produce 600 volt direct current electricity which, in turn, drove electric traction motors to turn the wheels. With an eight and one-half inch bore and ten inch stroke, each cylinder had a displacement of 567 cubic inches, giving the name to the series. Each downstroke of the diesel's pistons was a power stroke and each upstroke was for compression of the fuel/air mixture for the next power stroke. The Roots blower was needed to clear the com-

bustion products from the cylinder and bring in fresh air to mix with the injected diesel fuel. It also contributed to the distinctive "growl" or "chant" that characterized EMD locomotives of the period. Although not by design, the geared drive train of Lionel's F3's offered the model train operator of the 40's and early 50's a sort of "Railsounds" long before the electronic era, when digitally simulated diesel sounds became commonplace.

In 1950, "Magne-Traction" was incorporated into the F3 and these units carried the catalog numbers of 2343 for the Santa Fe and 2344 for the New York Central. The Santa Fe units were offered with the "top of the line" passenger sets through the years but a close look at the rear of the roofs reveals that there are no steam generator stacks or vents. Ironically Lionel's F3's were all technically "freight only" as steam generators were a necessity in those years for a prototype diesel to handle passenger trains. (The steam was needed to heat the cars and supply the dining car kitchens.) By contrast, the later Lionel GP7 models did have the steam generator details.

All of the Lionel F3's had the rectangular roof slots that indicated the presence of dynamic brakes. On a real diesel so equipped, the traction motors that turn the wheels on level and upgrade track, act as generators to hold back a train when descending hills and the energy they generate is dissipated as heat through resistor grids and fans on the locomotive's roof.

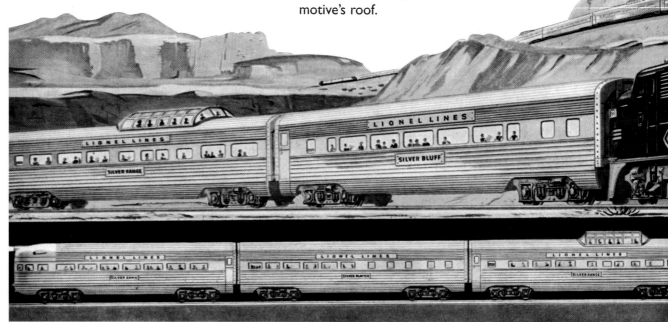

Page 20 & 21 of the 1952 Lionel Catalog.

Until 1953, the roof openings on the model were covered with fine metal screening that looked very much like the dynamic brake fan openings on a real F3. The F3 was a popular 1500 h.p. freight and passenger engine that was bought by many railroads in the United States as well as in Canada and Mexico. Understandably, the capable marketing staff at Lionel saw the possibilities of additional sales if its model could be offered in the color schemes of railroads in other parts of the country.

In 1952, the Western Pacific F3, catalog No. 2345 made its debut in the silver and orange passenger colors. It was mechanically identical to the No. 2343 Santa Fe F3. Despite the role of the real diesels in pulling the well-publicized CALIFORNIA ZEPHYR, sales apparently did not meet expectations, so the unit disappeared from the catalog by 1954. Its marketplace shortcomings had nothing to do with its collectible appeal or value in subsequent years. Its rarity and attractive color scheme make it a most welcome addition to any Lionel diesel collection.

The author occasionally assembled a truncated CALIFORNIA ZEPHYR of sorts by operating a pair of WP cab units with a train of 2530 series aluminum streamlined baggage cars, dome cars, coaches and observation car. While the train was short and Lionel never made a dome observation car, it captured the essence of the Salt Lake City to San Francisco segment of the ZEPHYR.

Also in 1952, Lionel added a "B" unit in Santa Fe and New York Central colors. Its body shell seemed to be made from a slightly modified version of the F3 "A" unit mold. The porthole and louvre pattern on its sides was identical to that used on the cab units, unlike the plain panels with three portholes on each side of the prototype F3's.

In the following year, Lionel's cost reduction resulted in the dynamic brake openings on the models' being represented by a series of short parallel slots molded directly into the units' roofs as a crude substitute for the metal screens. This simplification continued on all subsequent F3's made by Lionel. The Santa Fe, New York Central and Western Pacific F3's became catalog Nos. 2353, 2354 and 2355, respectively.

In 1954, Lionel introduced an A-B-A F3 in a quite accurate reproduction of the attractive gold trimmed green and white color scheme of the Southern Railway. Sales of this model locomotive were apparently disappointing, so it did not appear in the following catalogs. This, of course, made the No. 2356 relatively difficult to find in later years and its collector value greatly exceeds that of the Santa Fe or New York Central F3's.

During the following four years, the Lionel F3's went through further simplification in the interest of production economics. The clear plastic porthole windows disappeared, replaced by circular indentations in the sides. The steps under the cab doors were also eliminated, and the truck sideframes appeared only in a black oxidized finish. The power trucks were redesigned with the motors placed vertically, driving a single worm gear on a cross shaft that was, in turn, connected to the driving axles by spur gears. Despite its more economical construction, this truck, which was used on Lionel's GP7 and rectifier electric models, was quite rugged and ran smoothly and quietly. The distinctive F3 growling sound, however, was gone.

The bright side of this era of the Lionel F3 was the rainbow of color schemes in which the units were issued. Baltimore & Ohio, Wabash, Milwaukee (the early gray with red "flame" stripes), Rio Grande, Canadian Pacific and, of course, more Santa Fe F3's graced the catalogs during those years. In addition, the colors of the Illinois Central and New Haven railroads, who actually never owned F3's,

graced the Lionel model cab units. The Illinois Central's only road cab units were the much longer E6, E7 and E8 passenger units in the brown and orange scheme while the New Haven owned mid-length dual powered units, the FL9's in colors quite different from Lionel's offering. In the opinion of many Lionel historians, drawings of an experimental New Haven color scheme became available to Lionel before the real locomotives appeared. This inspired the appearance of the New Haven F3 which the company apparently wished to introduce in its catalog as soon as possible. Most of these models like the New Haven units were offered for relatively short periods and are also among those most sought after by Lionel train collectors. The author would have preferred to see a version of these units in the real New Haven FL9 colors and would have operated them extensively with approximations of the passenger trains he saw and photographed, but Lionel never saw fit to produce such a model.

In the final years of Lionel Corporation production, only the ubiquitous Santa Fe F3 remained in the catalog with the number 2383. It would remain to the succeeding manufacturer, the Model Products Corporation (MPC), a subsidiary of General Mills, to introduce new varieties and some re-issued versions of the 1950's F3 color schemes.

Color photographs of prototype F3's in service on the Santa Fe, New York Central, Rio Grande and many other railroads can be seen in the various hard cover books published by Morning Sun Books.

West Shore freight VW-6 passes through Dumont, New Jersey in February 1957 behind a pair of New York Central F3's that strongly resemble the head end power on Lionel's top of the line freight sets of the early 1950's. *(Robert Malinoski photo)*

Another pair of New York Central F3's are proceeding to their next assignment at Ann Arbor, Michigan in August 1963. One variation from the Lionel model is the black carbody with light gray lightning stripes.
(Emery Gulash photo)

Lionel's No. 2354 illustrates how well the company reproduced the New York Central F3 consistent with mass production necessities and the 31-inch circles it was designed to negotiate. *(William J. Brennan collection)*

The depiction of the No. 2344 New York Central F3 on page 25 in the company's 1952 catalog shows that the customer got what he or she expected.

The Wabash never owned any F3's but did rely heavily on the slightly newer EMD F7. Here, Wabash F7 685 leads a westbound freight through Jacksonville, Illinois on July 9, 1962. *(Dave Ingles photo, Lou Schmitz collection)*

No. 2240 . . . now in "027" gauge!
1956 Lionel Catalog, page 15

Wabash F7 700 leads a circus train through Hannibal, Missouri on August 22, 1961.
Generally, one can differentiate between an F3 and and F7 by the roofline grilles. F3's had rough screens (nicknamed "chicken wire") while F7's had smooth horizontal stainless steel grilles. The diesel purist will warn however of late model Phase IV F3's with smooth grilles. *(Dick Wallin photo, Lou Schmitz collection)*

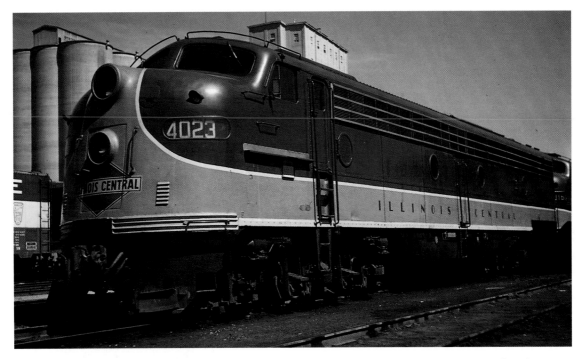

Illinois Central E8 4023 at Oak Street, East St. Louis, Illinois, illustrates the elegant passenger color scheme of chocolate and orange on a clear Spring day in May 1962. While the railroad did not operate any F units, Lionel adapted the colors to its F3's in 1955. *(Tom Smart photo, Bill Volkmer collection)*

IC E9 4041 was a May 1957 rebuild from an E7. The E7 had 2000 hp; the E8 2250 hp; and the E9 2400 hp. The 4041 is outside Chicago in August 1970. The road had by then eliminated the green diamond logo on the head end substituting a "split rail" IC. *(R.J. Yanosey collection)*

Electro-Motive's passenger diesels, in addition to proving more durable and reliable than those of their competitors, earned a reputation for high speed and smooth riding qualities. The company's advertisements, understandably, reflected these qualities. *(Robert J. Yanosey collection)*

Lionel depicted its Illinois Central F3's on *page 26* of its *1956 catalog.*

Milwaukee F7 75A and companions are less than a year old as they head up a long freight train in 1950. These were among the last units delivered in the flamboyant "flame stripe" color scheme, which apparently caught Lionel's fancy for its F3's of 1956. *(George Krambles photo)*

Majestic "O" gauge two-unit twin-motored diesel
The "Milwaukee"
1956 Lionel Catalog, page 22

Milwaukee F7 88A was photographed by Russ Porter of MODEL RAILROADER in the magazine's headquarters city of Milwaukee, Wisconsin. The Milwaukee's F-units would soon begin to wear a new paint scheme of an orange body and maroon stripe as new units arrived and older units were repainted. *(W. F. Strauss collection)*

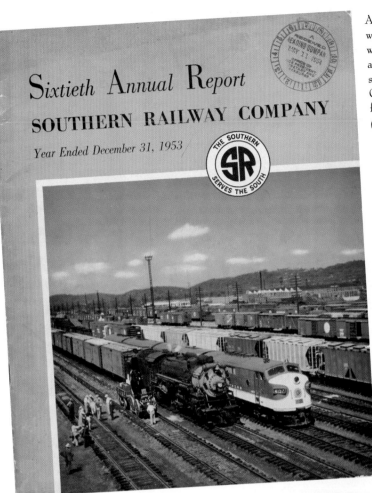

Another color scheme that appeared on Lionel's F3's was the dramatic green and white Southern RR scheme with gold trim stripes. On June 17, 1953 the Southern achieved complete dieselization and posed its last active steamer #6330 and a replica of the Best Friend of Charleston alongside one of its F3's. The road chose to feature the photo on its 1953 Annual Report cover. *(R.J. Yanosey collection)*

Page 26, 1956 Lionel Catalog.

In the late 1950's, the Southern switched to a more utilitarian paint scheme substituting black for the green. The Southern had some F3's which lasted quite beyond the time when most roads had already traded them in for new GP30's and GP40's. This is black F3 #4135 at the Ivy City engine terminal in Washington DC in May 1970 awaiting its assignment to a fast mail train. *(Bill Volkmer collection)*

The fidelity of the colors applied to Lionel's No. 2379 F3 in 1958 is confirmed by this view of Rio Grande 5654, an F7 seen at Grand Junction, Colorado in March 1965. *(Robert J. Yanosey collection)*

No. 2379 Two Motor "Rio Grande" *1958 Lionel Catalog, page 35*

This Electro-Motive advertisement described the diesels that it sold the Burlington, Rio-Grande and Western Pacific for use on the Chicago-San Francisco CALIFORNIA ZEPHYR. *(Robert J. Yanosey collection)*

In Oakland, California in 1949, Western Pacific F3's led by 803 await their next eastbound run on Train 18, the CALI-FORNIA ZEPHYR through the Feather River Canyon and on to Salt Lake City, Utah. *(Stephen D. Bogen photo)*

Pages 24 and 25 of the 1952 Lionel Catalog illustrate the No.2345 Western Pacific F3's.

The Western Pacific's 1949 Annual Report proudly portrayed its flagship CALIFORNIA ZEPHYR in the Feather River Canyon near Pulga, California. *(Robert J. Yanosey collection)*

After the end of World War II, the Missouri-Kansas-Texas Railroad (the KATY) and the
St. Louis-San Francisco Railway (the Frisco) ordered two sets of EMD E7 passenger diesels for their jointly operated
TEXAS SPECIAL which operated between St. Louis, Missouri and San Antonio, Texas.
One of the units, 101, is pictured here at Greenville, Texas in May 1947 showing the striking, attractive
combination of stainless steel panels with red and yellow paint. (Arthur G. Charles photo)

Understandably, Lionel chose not to undergo the tooling expense of creating an E7 passenger diesel
locomotive that would be too long for its tinplate tracks. Instead, the company skillfully modified the
color scheme by using white painted panels on red F3 carbodies with silver trucks, capturing the
distinctive appearance of the TEXAS SPECIAL for its 1955 version.

The Katy did own a dozen F3 units however, which were built by EMD in 1947. From this mid-1950's view in
Kansas City, MO you can see that the Lionel model was not far off the mark even though the Katy's F units had no
paint or other connection with THE TEXAS SPECIAL. (Carl Hehl photo, Lou Schmitz collection)

The New Haven RR never purchased the EMD F3 (or the FT, F7, or F9 for that matter) but by the mid 1950's was seeking a dual diesel/electric locomotive that would be housed in the standard EMD F-unit carbody. The unique locomotive was in development for quite a while. In this photo, New Haven FL9 5048 leads a New York-bound passenger train through Glenbrook, Connecticut in March 1970. *(Don Ball collection)*

Lionel apparently used one of a number of color schemes proposed for use on the New Haven's planned fleet of FL9's, as illustrated on *pages 28 and 29* of the *1958 catalog.*

New Haven FL9 5016 speeds along the mainline through Connecticut on a sunny June day in 1970. Lionel would certainly have had an appealing product had it chosen this paint scheme. *(Don Ball collection)*

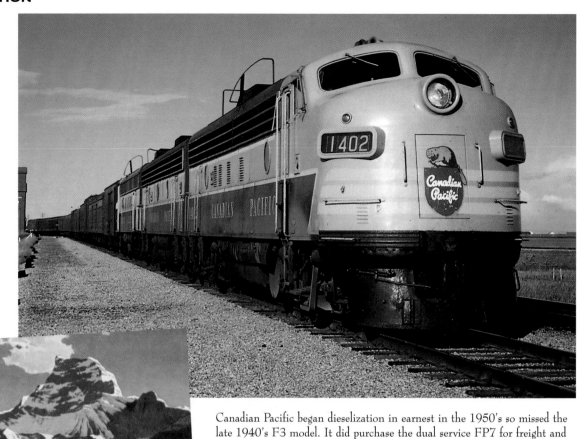

Canadian Pacific began dieselization in earnest in the 1950's so missed the late 1940's F3 model. It did purchase the dual service FP7 for freight and passenger service in 1954. Here, Canadian Pacific FP7 1402 leads two other units with the 25 cars of Train #7 THE DOMINION through Kemnay, Manitoba on June 18, 1960. *(G.M. Leilich photo)*

A Budd company advertisement of the mid-1950's shows the consist of the Canadian Pacific's CANADIAN passing through the Canadian Rockies. *(Robert J. Yanosey collection)*

A Budd-built Dome observation car brings up the rear of Train #7 at Calgary, Alberta in June 1960. *(G.M. Leilich photo)*

B&O did purchase the EMD F3, dieselizing most of its road freights with various models of F-units. Baltimore & Ohio look-alike F7 4559 and two trailing units lead a freight through Washington, D.C. in March 1961. (Edward S. Miller photo)

The Baltimore & Ohio Railroad, like many others, used colorful, artistically designed matchbooks as promotional items for their passengers or freight shippers to keep the company's image in sight. (Robert J. Yanosey collection)

Pages 22 and 23 of the 1956 Lionel Catalog illustrate the company's introduction of its Baltimore & Ohio F3's.

LIONEL
O TRAINS
plus
MAGNE-
TRACTION

Magnificent realism and Super-power

LIONEL Nos. 2227W AND 2229W "O" GAUGE 5-CAR FREIGHT

Choice of Twin-unit Santa Fe or N.Y.C. Diesels with Two Worm-Drive Motors, Built-in Horn and MAGNE-TRACTION

GOLDEN WEST SPECIAL and New York Central **WATER LEVEL LIMITED** — East or West these big "growlers" are champion freight handlers. Both these twin-unit Diesel locos are equipped with two motors and *MAGNE-TRACTION*. Both the New York Central and Santa Fe freights have identical car combinations. Included are the A.T. & S.F. remote control operating barrel car, NYC's yellow stock car, Lehigh Valley hopper, blue B&O automobile car and illuminated caboose. These freights measure 6 ft., 5 ins., long. Track oval is 70" by 31⅞". When ordering, specify train number. New York Central is 2229W, Santa Fe is 2227W.

Lionel Nos. 2227W Santa Fe and 2229W New York
Central 5-Car Freight Sets Comprise:
1 No. 2353 Santa Fe or 2354 New York Central Power Unit
1 No. 2353 Santa Fe or 2354 New York Central Motorless Unit
1 No. 3362 New Operating Barrel Car and Bin
1 No. 6356 New Scale-Modelled Stock Car
1 No. 6456 Hopper Car
1 No. 6468 Scale-Modelled Automobile Car
1 No. 6417 Illuminated Caboose
8 sec. OC Curved Track
7 sec. OS Straight Track
1 UCS Track Set
Lockon, Lubricant and
Instruction Booklet

For fuller details on the new Operating Barrel Car No. 3562 (above) see page 33.

Each $69.50
Set

24

While the various F3's for Milwaukee, Southern, Illinois Central and other roads are sought after collector items today, the two Lionel F3's most remembered are those painted for New York Central and even more, the Santa Fe. Both F3's were reliable and powerful. Indeed there are certainly Santa Fe and New York Central F3's built by Lionel out there that have been seen in yearly operation now for nearly half a century. Ironically, that's a lot more service life than the actual prototypes saw since most of them were constructed in 1947-1949 and were traded in on newer diesel models by the mid-1960's - a mere fifteen year lifetime.

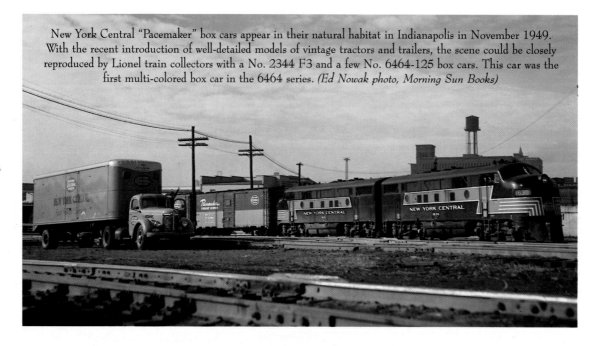

New York Central "Pacemaker" box cars appear in their natural habitat in Indianapolis in November 1949. With the recent introduction of well-detailed models of vintage tractors and trailers, the scene could be closely reproduced by Lionel train collectors with a No. 2344 F3 and a few No. 6464-125 box cars. This car was the first multi-colored box car in the 6464 series. *(Ed Nowak photo, Morning Sun Books)*

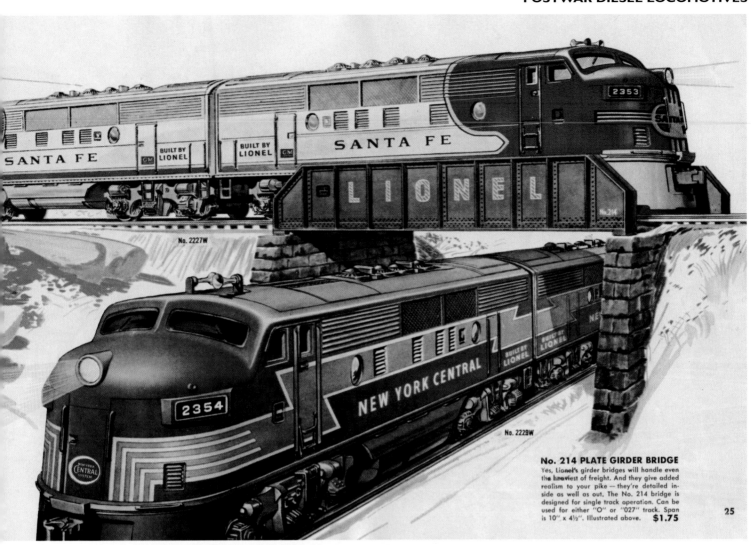

No. 214 PLATE GIRDER BRIDGE

Yes, Lionel's girder bridges will handle even the heaviest of freight. And they give added realism to your pike — they're detailed inside as well as out. The No. 214 bridge is designed for single track operation. Can be used for either "O" or "027" track. Span is 10" x 4½". Illustrated above. **$1.75**

25

Illustration from pages 24-25 of the 1954 Lionel catalog.

Santa Fe F7 310 traverses famous Cajon Pass in California's San Gabriel Mountains in August 1972. Such a scene could be faithfully reproduced using Lionel F3's and *Silver Cloud* cars. *(William J. Brennan photo)*

THE EMD 1000 H.P. SWITCHER

After the conclusion of World War II, during which EMD was restricted to producing road diesel locomotives, the company resumed marketing its line of diesel switching locomotives, including the NW2, powered by a 12 cylinder 567 series normally aspirated (not supercharged) 1000 h.p. diesel engine and found many customers among the nation's class I railroads. In 1949, Lionel introduced a quite realistic model of this switcher in the earliest markings of the Santa Fe Railroad, black with the railroad's initials in white along the upper sides of the hood, with its blue and white herald at the center. The Lionel locomotive, with either Nos. 622 or 6220, was sturdily constructed with a die cast frame and plastic body. The only major variation from exact scale proportions was the slight elongation of the cab to accommodate the motor. It was propelled by a well-designed and quiet running power truck with a vertically mounted motor that drove a transverse worm gear shaft that drove the powered axles through spur gears. This model also represented the quiet introduction of "Magne-Traction", which magnetized the driving wheels and greatly enhanced its pulling power. This power truck, which was used in subsequent versions of the NW2 and the "027" Alco FA-2's, introduced in 1950, is regarded by many Lionel train collectors and operators as the smoothest running power truck ever

made by the company. In 1952, the NW2 appeared in the attractive Chesapeake & Ohio blue color scheme with yellow frame striping. In 1954, a Seaboard version was introduced in an unusual blue and orange color scheme that never used by that road, to the author's knowledge. Lionel's design staff was apparently favorably impressed with the Tangerine and blue used on the Jersey Central's early road diesel locomotives and used it on the Seaboard switcher as well as a Jersey Central NW2 and Train Master. Lionel later produced a Seaboard NW2 in the correct red and black color scheme, although with a sheet metal frame and a much less substantial fabricated sheet metal power truck. These later trucks featured the "Blomberg" side frames similar to those used on the F3 and GP7, rather than the correct AAR sideframes used on the earlier NW2 models. This later version of the diesel switcher was also offered in fairly accurate versions of the Erie, Katy and Union Pacific color schemes.

Most diesel switchers did not need dynamic brakes, but the option was available for buyers who intended to haul heavy consists on steep grades. The dynamic brake was installed in a square housing immediately ahead of the cab. Additional air reservoirs were also available for applications where frequent and extensive braking was expected. Lionel featured both of these options in its 1959-60 Alaska Railroad NW2 by adding a yellow plastic reproduction of the dynamic brake housing and air reservoirs ahead of the cab of the dark blue carbody.

Santa Fe NW2 2408 represents the color scheme applied to the railroad's switchers and roadswitchers after World War II. It was photographed at Chicago, Illinois on March 1, 1966. From 1948 to 1954, Lionel may have chosen the prewar solid black scheme without striping to economize production. By 1961, the painting and lettering technology had advanced and Lionel produced the No. 616 Santa Fe switcher with striping nearly identical to the prototype. *(Karl C. Henkels photo, R.J. Yanosey collection)*

Page 30 of Lionel's 1954 catalog illustrates the No. 623 Santa Fe and the No. 624 Chesapeake & Ohio NW2 switchers.

This example of Lionel's No. 623 diesel switcher survived the decades well. The author was fortunate to acquire it with its original box in 1966. *(William J. Brennan collection)*

Chesapeake & Ohio NW2 5068 displays a color scheme quite similar to Lionel's in Detroit, Michigan in June, 1978.
(David Hamley photo, William J. Brennan collection)

ACTION EVERY SPIK
"UNION PACIFIC" WOR

NEW! No. 613

UNION PACIFIC

SERVES ALL
THE WEST
613

No. 6476

LV
64766
CAPY
LD LMT

LEHIGH VALLEY

LV

No. 602

SEABOARD

602

No. 111

No. 611

JERSEY CENTRAL
611

LIONEL'S No. 1593 "027" 5-CA
HEADLIGHT • MAGNE-TRACTION

High . . . high above the wandering river she zooms . . . a streak of color
against the sky! Every line has a train like this rugged work train.
The headlight-equipped diesel at the front carries the famous colors
and markings of the Union Pacific. Lift and lower freight with the amazing new boom car. Look at the new flat car with a realistic transformer
lashed on top. Look at the hopper car . . . the gondola with removable
canisters . . . the work caboose. Train measures 4 ft., 10½ ins. long.

No. 1015
45-WATT TRANSFORMER
included with train set.

AVAILABLE FOR
SEPARATE SALE

6   For items not described,
see index page 45.

NEW! No. 613 Union Pacific Diesel—
Equipped with powerful Magne-Traction, bril-
liant headlight, self-centering couplers front
and rear. A versatile road switcher based on
GM's 125-ton "NW2". Loco 12¼" long. $21.50

No. 602 Seaboard Diesel—A
"jack of all trades" switcher with
real-sounding built-in diesel horn,
headlight, track-hugging Magne-
Traction. Loco 12¼" long. $27.50

No. 611 Jersey Central Diesel—
A rugged roustabout for yard work or
main line. Has powerful headlight and
exclusive Lionel Magne-Traction. Loco
12¼" long. $21.50

No. 6476 Hopper Car—Just like
coal hoppers seen on every eastern railroad. Blazoned with
famous Lehigh Valley signature.
Car 9⅜" long. $3.50

NEW! No. 6818 Flat Car with Transformer—As modern a sight as you'll see
anywhere! Powerful-looking simulated
transformer sits astride this 11" long
flat car . . . can be removed. $4.95

Pages 6 and 7 of the 1958 Lionel catalog depicts three variations of the sheet metal frame
NW2's, No. 613 Union Pacific, No. 602 Seaboard and No. 611 Jersey Central.

The "economy" version of the Lionel NW2 appeared in 1955 with the No. 610 Erie switcher in a fairly
realistic black with a skeletal Erie Railroad diamond in yellow. The company's use of a drab color scheme
on a diesel model probably accounted for this model appearing for only one year. The prototype's
full herald and yellow body and frame stripes as shown on Erie's 401 at Hoboken in January 1966 would
have considerably enhanced the otherwise all black model. (William J. Brennan photo)

F THE WAY...
AIN No. 1593

ION PACIFIC" DIESEL WORK TRAIN $35.00

TRANSFORMER and BOOM CARS

1593 Train Set includes:	If bought separately		If bought separately
613 New "Union Pacific" Diesel Switcher	$21.50	8 Sections No. 1013 Curved Track	2.00
6476 Hopper Car	3.50	2 Sections No. 1018 Straight Track	.50
6818 New Flat Car with Transformer	4.95	No. 1008 Automatic Uncoupling Control	1.50
6660 New Boom Car	6.95	No. 1015 45-Watt Transformer	6.95
6112 Gondola with Canisters	3.50	CTC Lockon	.25
6119 Work Caboose	3.50	Lubricant and Instruction Sheet.	

W! No. 6660 Boom Car—The "big hook"! Exciting
l manual controls let you (1) raise or lower hook and
actually raise or lower the boom itself. Unique out-
ers steady car when boom swivels out with heavy
ds. Car 11" long. $6.95

NEW! No. 321 Trestle Bridge—Easy-to-
assemble model of Pennsylvania-type railroad bridge. Has steel base and molded
details, perfect to the last rivet. Bridge
4½" wide, 24" long, 7" high. $4.95

No. 111 Trestle Set — 10
sturdy, realistic piers. May be
used with No. 110 Graduated
Trestle Set to extend an elevated
line. Each pier 4¾" high. $3.95

No. 110 Graduated Trestle Set — 24
graduated piers for use with locos equipped
with Magne-Traction. Piers 3/16" to 4¾"
in height. High point provides clearance for
train to pass underneath. $5.95

You can set up this interesting
track arrangement by using
Lionel's Nos. 110 and 111
Trestle Sets.

Many of these scenic effects
can be made with Lionel's No.
920 Scenic Display Kit.

7

When Lionel created its Jersey Central NW2 1000 hp. diesel switcher in 1956, the carbody was dark blue plastic with orange lettering and emblems. The prototype, as the photo of 1061 in May 1976 at Elizabethport, New Jersey indicates, continued to wear a utilitarian coat of Sea Green with yellow numbers and lettering, probably considered to be too drab by the company's marketing people. A number of Jersey Central switchers were repainted between 1969 and 1972 in Baltimore & Ohio-inspired dark blue carbodies with yellow lettering, emblems and framestripes, nearly recreating Lionel's earlier interpretation. *(William J. Brennan photo)*

Between shifts of switching freight cars in East Los Angeles, Union Pacific NW2 1039 idles in the engine terminal on August 21, 1978. *(William J. Brennan photo)*

85

In 1959, the dynamic brake-equipped No. 614 Alaska Railroad diesel switcher appeared with an "027" freight set. A few EMD switchers on real railroads were equipped with dynamic brakes, such as the West Virginia Northern and the Lehigh Valley, whose SW8 266 is shown at Bethlehem, Pennsylvania in March 1976. The feature was used when the units handled heavy cuts of cars on steep grades. Interestingly enough, The Alaska Railroad did not have any switchers so equipped. *(William J. Brennan photo)*

Actually, dynamic brake-equipped switchers were quite rare. Another road using them for ambling up and down coal branches was the West Virginia Northern. Here WVN SW1200 #52 sits near the Baltimore & Ohio interchange at Tunnelton, West Virginia in July 1969. EMD switchers with dynamic brakes were also purchased by Coos Bay Lumber Co., Canadian Forest Products, Southern Pacific and Union Pacific. *(William J. Brennan photo)*

THE ALCO FA 2

During World War II, The War Production Board gave the Electro-Motive Division (EMD) of General Motors the exclusive right to manufacture diesel road locomotives and the other builders, Alco and Baldwin, were assigned the diesel switcher market. In 1946, Alco began to produce its first road freight diesel, the FA-1 which was powered by a 1500 h.p. turbocharged 12 cylinder 244 series engine with a nine inch bore and ten and one-half inch stroke. In 1950, the design was modified slightly and the output increased to 1600 h.p. The most visible change was moving the circular rooftop fan and side radiator shutters about four feet forward from the rear of the carbody.

Possibly in deference to EMD, Lionel's version of the FA-2 was not reproduced in nearly full scale but about 20% smaller, to match the company's smaller and lower priced "027" line of equipment. Lionel's 1950 creation captured the overall appearance and proportions of the real Alco freight diesel units in the model's plastic shell and die-cast zinc alloy chassis, and propelled the "027" model with a powerful, smooth-running power truck used earlier in its NW2 diesel switcher. In that year, the feature of "Magne-Traction" first appeared, significantly increasing the pulling power of locomotives so equipped. The model, carrying catalog number 2023, carried a reasonably accurate rendition of the attractive Armour Yellow and gray colors of the Union Pacific Railroad.

The FA-2 appeared with Union Pacific lettering and heralds on a non-prototypical silver scheme with a gray roof in 1951 and in solid silver in 1952. The latter year also saw the introduction of attractive versions in Rock Island's red and black scheme and a slightly simplified rendition of Erie's familiar black with yellow trim striping and diamond emblems. These diesels remained in the catalog until 1954, and are desirable collectibles.

The Alco freight cab unit would not reappear until the period from 1957 to 1963, as a "dressed down" economy version with simplified plastic body shells, sheet metal frames and skeletal power trucks that were far less substantial than those used between 1950 and 1954. These units appeared most frequently in the lower priced sets. The company used a variety of mostly non-prototypical color schemes attributed to the Santa Fe, Missouri Pacific, Boston & Maine, Minneapolis & St. Louis railroads, and the TEXAS SPECIAL, most of which never owned any real FA's. One exception was the New Haven, catalog number 209 that carried a quite realistic red, black and white McGinnis color scheme that, in the author's opinion, was the most attractive of the series. Unfortunately, the 209 appeared in only one year, 1958. An interesting addition to the economy version of the "027" Alco road diesel in the late 1950's was a companion "B" or booster unit.

The cover of the 1947 Erie Railroad Annual Report illustrates the pride that the company took in its newly-acquired Alco FA-1 freight diesels. *(Robert J. Yanosey collection)*

Lionel's No. 2032 FA-2 displayed the somewhat spartan striping given the Erie Railroad's first diesel freight units, EMD FT's delivered during World War II. The Erie's other postwar freight diesels showed a more generous use of yellow on the cab and around the winged nose emblem as this photo of Erie 7214 at Hammond, Indiana in August 1961, illustrates.

(Bill Volkmer photo)

In 1947, newly acquired Union Pacific FA-1 1500A and FB-1 1524 made their trial run and posed for the company photographer. They compared favorably with the EMD counterpart, the 1500 hp F3, so the UP ordered a total of eighty FA's. (UPRR Museum - KDFT423)

Lionel's Erie and Union Pacific FA-2's appear with freight and passenger trains, respectively, on *pages 8 and 9* in the company's *1952 catalog.*

Rock Island FA-1 158 poses for a publicity photo in the granger territory
that generated a substantial share of the railroad's traffic. *(Don Ball collection)*

Page 24 of the 1952 Lionel catalog

Over 20 years had passed since Rock Island FA-1 130 arrived on the property when the locomotive was
photographed at Blue Island, Illinois on May 8, 1968. Alas, the Alco prime mover was not the equal of its
EMD rival so the unit had been re-engined in the mid 1950's with a GM 567C diesel. A new simplified
paint scheme was also used. *(Karl C. Henkels photo, R.J. Yanosey collection)*

In 1959, Lionel produced two Santa Fe variations of the Alco FA-2, No. 218 in the road's red and silver "Warbonnet" passenger color scheme color scheme and No. 208 in the blue and yellow freight colors as shown from *page 12* of the *1959 catalog.*

Lionel's application of Santa Fe freight colors to Alco FA-2's was an exercise in the type of artistic license that occurs frequently in the toy and model train industry. The only road cab and booster units that the Santa Fe used in freight service were Electro-Motive FT, F3, F7, and F9's like F7 266C seen here at Clovis, New Mexico on March 3, 1970. Several of the 260-series F7's were delivered during the Korean War in 1951 with F3-like "chicken wire" instead of stainless steel grilles. *(Karl C. Henkels photo)*

The only Alco cab units that the Santa Fe operated were a fleet of PA-1's used in passenger service, typified by No. 74, shown at Barstow, California on November 30, 1968. This was undoubtedly the inspiration for the Lionel 218. *(Robert J. Yanosey collection)*

In its efforts to expand the geographic appeal of its electric trains, Lionel produced
a Missouri Pacific FA-2 in 1957 and 1958. An example of the prototype, the road's No. 376
awaits its next train at Omaha, Nebraska on August 7, 1960. *(Lou Schmitz photo)*

Lionel's No. 205 Missouri Pacific FA-2's represented the railroad's simplified solid blue color
scheme as they appeared on *page 10* of the company's *1958 catalog.*

Missouri Pacific FA-2 382 wears a recently-applied solid blue color scheme at North Little Rock, Arkansas
on July 10, 1961. This actually was more like the Lionel 205. *(Lou Schmitz collection)*

The New Haven later applied a dignified and more serviceable paint scheme of Hunter Green with yellow striping illustrated by the 0415 at Maybrook, New York, the western extremity of the railroad. *(Al Holtz)*

New Haven's first FA-1's were delivered in an attractive orange and green color scheme with silver trim striping as demonstrated by 0402 at New Haven in 1950 during a railfan visit. *(Stephen D. Bogen photo)*

Page 18 of the *1958 Lionel catalog* displayed its No. 209 New Haven FA-2's in the early McGinnis color scheme with eye-catching geometric patterns of vermilion, black and white. The prototype diesel colors were later modified to move the white side color band to the top to minimize the effect of road grime.

The later version of the McGinnis colors is shown on 0424 at New Haven, Connecticut in July, 1963. Note that the white is now on the nose of the unit. *(Don Ball collection)*

THE FAIRBANKS-MORSE TRAIN MASTER

In 1953, Fairbanks-Morse introduced its famous TRAIN MASTER diesel locomotive that produced 2400 h.p., making it the most powerful single-engined roadswitcher of its time. An opposed-piston engine has upper and lower crankshafts, which are geared together. These in-line engines have no cylinder heads; the pistons approach each other on the compression stroke and move in opposite directions on the power stroke. Like the EMD diesels, they were two cycle engines which yielded more power for their size than the four cycle engines used by other builders. These engines first gained fame as the power plants of about half of America's World War II submarines as well as other naval vessels. Two Train Masters could handle the work of three smaller roadswitchers such as GP7's. The tall carbody (necessitated by the height of the opposed-piston power plant), 66 foot length and the low pitched drumming of

the engine when pulling or accelerating a train, conveyed the essence of mass and power. These units never seemed to be straining, even while handling the heaviest trains. During the late 1950's, the author heard an older railroad fan, who frequently and vocally lamented the passing of the steam locomotive, describe the Train Master as the only diesel for which he had any respect. The prototype locomotives were initially used by the Jersey Central, Lackawanna, Reading and the Southern Pacific railroads mainly for commuter and suburban passenger service. The other owners, the Southern, Virginian, Wabash and Pennsylvania railroads used them primarily on freight trains.

Lionel capitalized on the abundant favorable publicity that the massive Train Masters generated and produced a very realistic model in 1954 as catalog No. 2321 in a reasonably accurate version of the attractive and maroon and gray colors of the Lackawanna Railroad, the first railroad to order these locomotives. The catalog illustrations showed the unit as having a gray roof, but the early production models sported

maroon roofs that more closely approximated the appearance of the real Lackawanna locomotives whose roofs were painted black, probably to minimize the discoloration of exhaust soot and weather. Later production No. 2321 Train Masters had gray roofs. At the time, the Lackawanna's newly acquired locomotives were handling commuter trains between Hoboken and Branchville, New Jersey and enjoyed high visibility in the New York metropolitan area. These factors probably influenced Lionel's choice of this road name. Unlike Lionel's practice with the F3 and GP7, the model Train Master was exactly proportioned without any reduction in height, probably because the prototype units towered noticeably over most contemporary diesel locomotives and rolling stock and Lionel may have chosen to emphasize this feature. The unit featured twin motors in newly designed power trucks that resembled the distinctive six wheeled trucks of the prototype. Each motor was mounted vertically and drove a single worm gear on a cross shaft that was connected to the center and inboard axles by a spur gear. The inboard axles (closest to the center of the unit) on Lionel's version had no flanges ("blind")

and were not geared to the motor. The purpose of this arrangement was to minimize the overhang of Lionel's largest diesel on the sharp "O" Gauge curves and eliminate the risk of the unit striking the housings on Lionel switches. This Lionel power truck ran quite smoothly and reliably and probably inspired the design used on the GP7 and the reassigned F3 a year later. The Train Master is still regarded by knowledgeable collectors to be the most powerful model diesel made by Lionel.

In 1955, Lionel introduced its second variation of the Train Master, catalog No. 2331, in the black and yellow colors of the Virginian Railway, a mid-sized carrier whose principal function was moving West Virginia coal to the tidewater area at Norfolk, Virginia. The earlier chapter on the Virginian rectifier locomotive contains a more detailed description of this obscure, but very interesting railroad.

The Virginian Train Master reappeared in the 1956 catalog as No. 2331 but with a blue basic body color instead of black. This variation from the actual Virginian color scheme was a exercise in artistic license by Lionel, apparently intended to make the model

Lionel's full scale sized model of the Fairbanks-Morse Train Master graced *pages 18 and 19* of the company's *1954 catalog.*

more appealing. This change was apparently successful as the Virginian Train Master outlasted its siblings in the company's catalog, being offered until 1958 and reappearing in 1965-66 as No. 2332. This production change, of course, rendered the Black and yellow version of the Virginian Train Master quite valuable to collectors. As an interesting historical note, the Virginian Railway bought the last prototype Train Masters to be built by Fairbanks-Morse.

In 1956, Lionel introduced its Jersey Central Train Master as catalog No. 2341 in an orange and blue color scheme that strongly resembled the pattern of colors used on the Virginian model. The Lionel model actually bore little resemblance to the prototype units on the Jersey Central. Since the early 1950's that railroad's diesel power, including its Train Masters, wore a Sea Green basic body color with yellow horizontal "toothpaste" striping along the sides, converging at yellow "Liberty Head" heralds on the ends. The Jersey Central had used an orange (known as "Tangerine" to serious CNJ historians) and blue color

The Lackawanna Railroad was the first road to purchase the FM Train Master using them in both heavy mountain freight service and New Jersey suburban runs. Here, no. 856 rests in Hoboken, N.J. on September 8, 1956 awaitng its next commuter run. *(Bob Krone photo)*

The author's well-preserved No. 2321 maroon top Lackawanna Train Master shows the care that Lionel exercised to reproduce this massive diesel in "O" gauge.

scheme on its first EMD and Baldwin road diesels of the mid-1940's and pictures of these units might have inspired Lionel's use of orange and blue on its model. The CNJ's first 1500 hp FM roadswitchers were painted blue with tangerine stripes. These may also have influenced the choice of colors on No. 2341. The company thus avoided what it considered to be an excessively drab color scheme (this was the year in which the colors of the Virginian model were changed). The CNJ model, despite the bright color scheme, did not meet sales expectations and was not offered subsequently. It is considered to be the rarest of the Lionel Train Masters and, consequently, the most valuable.

An authentic Lionel model of the Jersey Central Train Master did not appear for another thirty years, when Lionel Trains, Inc. introduced its No. 8687 in the correct sea green color scheme with yellow striping in 1986. These models brought back fond memories for the author who owns two, which he operates regularly on long freight trains, much as the prototype railroad often dispatched a pair of Train Masters on a train which would otherwise require three F3 units. The author's memories of Jersey Central's Train Masters were reinforced in 1990 and 1992, when he wrote *Jersey Central Lines - In Color*, Volumes 1 and 2 (also from Morning Sun Books) and, in the process, enjoyed examining in detail many 1960's vintage color slides of these monsters at work.

Lionel added a Virginian Train Master in 1955 in black and yellow colors. By the following year, the base color was changed to blue, as this art from *page 16* of the *1956 Lionel catalog* shows.

Virginian Train Master 167 is the property of the Norfolk and Western as it and a repainted fellow unit proceed through Alloy, West Virginia in May 1963 with a freight train short enough to appear on the pages of a 1950's Lionel catalog. *(Bill Volkmer photo)*

The bright tangerine and blue colors of Jersey Central F3 55, shown here at Jersey City in August 1955, were adapted by Lionel in an effort to make the No. 2341 Train Master more attractive to prospective buyers than a Sea Green unit. *(Walter E. Zullig, Jr. photo)*

Jersey Central Train Master 2405 awaited its next assignment on an eastbound passenger train in Allentown, Pennsylvania in September 1961. The Sea Green carbody with Imitation Gold striping was apparently not sufficiently colorful for the marketing staff at Lionel. *(Matthew J. Herson, Jr. photo)*

THE
ELECTRO-MOTIVE
GP7

In 1949, The Electro-Motive Division of General Motors (EMD) responded to the demands of the railroad industry for a general purpose (hence the model designation) diesel locomotive. For a number of years, EMD's competitors already offered and sold a variety of general purpose roadswitcher models, but the superior reputation of EMD's road freight and passenger diesels, like the F3, caused some railroad motive power managers to prod EMD to make an all-purpose utility unit. After some earlier models that could be considered experimental in nature, the first GP7 with its angular lines made its debut in 1949. It possessed a similar two-cycle 16 cylinder power plant to that used in the F3 and F7 and also generated 1500 h.p. The unit was an instant success and soon surpassed its competitors in reliability, low maintenance costs and, consequently, sales.

Lionel recognized the sales potential that the prototype GP7 inspired and, in 1955, introduced models in Burlington, Milwaukee Road and Pennsylvania Railroad colors. All of the units used a newly developed power truck with a vertically mounted motor similar to that introduced on the F3's that year, which provid-

ed smooth, reliable operation. The Lionel model had a well-detailed plastic shell and a heavy sheet metal floor. The side handrails were made of punched out sheet metal spot-welded to the floor. The front railings were similarly fabricated and riveted to the ends of the floor. While these parts were far thicker than scale size, they provided needed ruggedness for the rough handling the engines were likely to encounter as playthings for the rambunctious young owners of their time.

The GP7's were equipped with the same battery operated horns that were used in the company's other diesel and electric locomotives of the period.

Overall, the Lionel GP7s looked quite realistic. Their overall dimensions were close to scale, with only the height slightly reduced, much like the F3. This was done to avoid having the locomotives dwarf the "027" size freight cars, cabooses and passenger cars that accompanied them in train sets. Another modest deviation from exact scale proportions was a slight addition to the cab length to accommodate the motor. Unlike the Lionel F3, the GP7 reflected a unit equipped with a steam generator, with the vent stack and top

General Motors took sufficient pride in its recently introduced GP7 roadswitcher that it advertised its new creation widely, as this display advertisement in the March 25, 1950 issue of the *Saturday Evening Post*. (*Robert J. Yanosey collection*)

of the steam boiler molded into the top of the short hood. The Milwaukee Road GP7, No. 2338, had a nearly correct version of the orange and black "Halloween" color scheme that adorned that railroad's switchers and roadswitchers. The only difference was that the sides of the Lionel unit's cab were solid black, while the real engines had the orange stripe across the portion below the windows. A small portion of Lionel's production run, however, did have the orange stripe like the prototype. These are quite rare and highly desired by Lionel diesel collectors. Interestingly enough, the prototype Milwaukee Road never owned a GP7, but had a substantial fleet of the similar looking succeeding EMD model, the GP9, which will be described later. Lionel also produced a Burlington GP7, No. 2328, with a silver body and red frame that bore no resemblance to the black and gray colors of the real CB&Q GP7's.

In the same year, a spartan Pennsylvania version, No. 2028, appeared with a body molded in maroon plastic with rubber stamped gold lettering. This model lacked headlight or number board lenses and the black plastic fuel tank which housed the flashlight batteries for the horns on the other GP7's. The real Pennsylvania Railroad GP7's were painted in the dark Brunswick Green (almost black) and were lettered in Dulux yellow in a manner similar to the Lionel offering.

The Lionel GP7 appeared in a number of other attractive color schemes, such as the Wabash and Chesapeake and Ohio. Some of the prototype GP7's were built with the dynamic brake option, similar to that in the F3s. While the equipment fitted easily into the F3 carbody, the confines of the narrow hood of the GP7 required the resistor grids to be placed in torpedo-shaped pods on each side of the long hood about half way between the cab and the end of the hood. By 1956, Lionel added fairly realistic dynamic brake pods to its units' roofs, but erred in calling the new variation a "GP9", probably because the dynamic brakes gave the units a "huskier" look. The GP9 was EMD's succeeding model, a 1750 horsepower unit that was introduced to the railroad industry in 1954. While its overall appearance was similar, the arrangement of the louvres on the sides of the long hood was considerably different. Instead of the two pairs of louvres near the cab with two others near the end of the long hood, there were three rows near the GP9's cab and only one near the end. Considering its role as a toymaker, Lionel cannot be criticized too loudly for this faux pas as a well-known manufacturer of fine HO scale trains, Athearn, made the same mistake for many years after its "GP9" was introduced in the mid-50's. A close look at their model reveals that it, too, is really a dynamic brake-equipped GP7.

In view of the Lionel catalog's description of its dynamic brake-equipped model roadswitcher as a "GP9" and the use of a different group of color schemes, these locomotives are described on page 105.

The author's Lionel No. 2338 GP7 has carried its 42 years of existence well, having been purchased in 1966 and reposing in his collection ever since. (William J. Brennan collection)

Pages 10 and 11 of the *1956 Lionel catalog* illustrate the newly-introduced No. 2338 Milwaukee Road GP7.

Milwaukee 207 poses with a commuter train in Deerfield, Illinois in April 1962. Unlike Lionel's No. 2338, this unit is a GP9 (the railroad never owned any GP7's). The solid black cab on most 2338's is the only exception to an otherwise accurate reproduction of the prototype's color scheme. There is actually a rare variation of this GP7 with the correct solid orange band going across the cab. *(Emery Gulash photo)*

Milwaukee 206 pulls a short commuter train near Union Station, Chicago, Illinois in February 1961. *(Emery Gulash photo)*

Burlington GP7 251 displays
its original color scheme at
Cicero, Illinois in May 1963.
*(Karl C. Henkels photo,
RJ Yanosey collection)*

Lionel probably produced its No. 2328
with a solid silver carbody because the
railroad's more highly publicized
passenger diesels were painted silver and
often included stainless steel body panels.
Prospective customers might have been
thought to expect a Burlington diesel to
be silver as illustrated by Burlington's
9952, an E5 at Amarillo, Texas with
Train No. 8 in May 1963.
(Emery Gulash photo)

Chesapeake & Ohio GP7 5772
displays its original color scheme
nearly intact at Chicago in
January 1973. Lionel produced
its verson, No. 2365, in 1962
with the prototype's later
simplified color scheme of a solid
blue carbody with yellow lettering
and frame. *(Bill Volkmer collection)*

Wabash GP7 452 awaits its next assignment at Fort Wayne, Indiana in
August 1963. Lionel's reproduction of this color scheme in its
No. 2337 and No. 2339 GP7's was quite accurate.
(Emery Gulash photo)

Lionel illustrated its
No. 2337 Wabash
GP7 on *page 14* of its
1958 catalog.

The long hood end of Wabash 472 at Chicago
March 16, 1965 shows that Lionel captured
the intricate paint scheme quite well.
(KC Henkels photo, R.J. Yanosey collection)

The PRR GP7 (2028) was produced in maroon by Lionel, Pennsy's actual passenger cab unit diesel color. The PRR GP7 was painted Brunswick Green but did see some passenger work. The versatility of the GP7 resulted in such assignments as helping westbound passenger trains around the Pennsylvania Railroad's Horse Shoe Curve, as the railroad's 8507 was doing in the early 1950's. *(Thomas J. MacNamara photo)*

A number of PRR GP7's were used for the Chicago-Valparaiso commuter run. Pennsylvania's 8501 leaves Chicago with a local train bound for Valparaiso, Indiana in 1963. *(J. J. Buckley photo)*

Most PRR GP7's soldiered on in local freight service. Here Pennsylvania GP7 5876 is ready for winter a bit early as it wears its snow plow at Altoona, Pennsylvania in August 1967. *(Martin Stanley Zak photo)*

THE LIONEL "GP9"

During the early 1950's, the automotive "horsepower race" was matched by the competitive increase in 1950 of the power of the roadswitcher models offered by EMD's rivals, Alco, Baldwin and Fairbanks-Morse to 1600 h.p. It took some time, but in 1954, EMD modified the design of its GP7 to produce 1750 h.p., temporarily leapfrogging the competition. The GP9 resembled the GP7 except for a different arrangement of the louvres on the sides of the long hood and on the battery boxes under the cab. Both models came with or without the dynamic brake pods on the roof, disproving the impression that only GP9's were so equipped. Most eastern roads, however, used their GP7's in local freight and commuter passenger train service where dynamic brakes were unnecessary. By contrast, the massive fleets of GP9's that displaced the last vestiges of steam on the Pennsylvania, Baltimore & Ohio and Norfolk and Western railroads came equipped with dynamic brakes in deference to the mountainous profiles they would face in heavy mainline freight service. Even some Northeastern regional roads like the New Haven received their GP9's with dynamic brakes. Understandably, the decision makers of Lionel, whether in Manhattan or Irvington/Hillside were probably influenced by the diesel locomotives they saw and the railroad trade journals they read and came away with the impression that the dynamic brake pods characterized the GP9 as opposed to the GP7 that lacked this feature. In view of the otherwise similar appearance of the prototype GP7's and GP9's, Lionel understandably did not see fit to modify the body mold to include the proper GP9 louvre patterns. The Lionel "GP9's" were, however, mechanically identical to the earlier GP7's and were equipped with the same motors, reverse relays and battery powered horns.

Lionel's first GP9 appeared in the Lionel catalog in 1958 as No. 2358 in the attractive red and white colors of the Minneapolis & St. Louis Railroad (M&StL). The almost obscure prototype railroad had lines radiating out of the Twin Cities of Minneapolis-St. Paul, which constituted the largest population center that it served. Its westernmost outpost was Leola, South Dakota, just west of Aberdeen and its closest approaches to St. Louis, Missouri were Peoria, Illinois or Albia, Iowa, where it made connections via the Wabash, Illinois Central and other lines to St. Louis. While Lionel usually used the color schemes of railroads in heavily populated areas for its models, this choice was clearly an exception. The appeal of the "Peoria Gateway" that introduced the

Lionel's 2359 closely resembles the Boston & Maine Railroad's first Second Generation diesels that not only replaced the fleet of wartime FT's and postwar F2's but introduced the Patrick McGinnis color scheme of the second railroad that he took over. *(William J. Brennan collection)*

M&StL in one of the first 6464 series boxcars may have influenced the company's selection.

In 1959, the Lionel GP9 was introduced in the black and gold colors of the Northern Pacific Railroad, apparently designed to appeal to potential customers in the northern Midwest and Pacific Northwest. Here, too, Lionel's No. 2349 was a fairly realistic version of its prototype.

By 1961, the GP9 model appeared in the attractive and quite authentic blue, black and white colors of the Boston & Maine Railroad as No. 2359. This Lionel locomotive reappeared briefly as No. 2346 in 1965. The prototype locomotives were among the earliest "second generation" diesels; they replaced the B&M's older EMD FT and F2 road freight units which were traded in for the new GP9's. During this time, the prototype locomotive builders offered a substantial credit toward the purchase of new units if the buyer returned obsolete units, particularly of the same make. In the case of the B&M, the older units, which somewhat resembled the F3's in overall appearance, has similar truck castings, traction motor construction and engine and electrical components that could be reconditioned and modified for use in the new locomotives. The fleet of blue GP9's soon went to work, primarily on heavy freights on the B&M's hilly east-west "Minute Man" route between Boston and Mechanicville, New York. The route crosses the Berkshire Mountains of western Massachusetts after which the famous 2-8-4 steam freight locomotives were named and includes the famous 4.25 mile long Hoosac Tunnel that was completed in 1875. Modellers wishing to simulate this operation should use two or three "GP9's" with a long freight consist. While the Lionel B&M square caboose is not an exact model of the type used on the real railroad, it is a reasonable approximation. The prototype of the articulated Lionel FLYING YANKEE train also ran over this route as a condensed version of the MINUTE MAN between Boston and Troy, New York, east of the Hudson River near Albany.

In April 1970, a Boston & Maine GP9 lays over at Mechanicville, New York, the western extremity of the railroad before bringing an eastbound freight over the "Minute Man Route" to Boston. The model, No. 2346 and No. 2359. *(R.J. Yanosey collection)*

Northern Pacific GP9 1756 is ready for assignment to a freight train at Livingston, Montana in August 1970. Lionel's 2349 is a quite accurate reproduction of the locomotive's color scheme. The only significant variation is Lionel's use of metallic gold as compared with the Dulux Gold on the prototype. *(William J. Brennan photo)*

Ten days after their delivery to the railroad, Minneapolis & St. Louis GP9's 702 and 709 are receiving sand in Peoria, Illinois in October 1958. That same year, Lionel introduced its No. 2348 with a color scheme that was right on target with its colorful prototype. The market for the unit was apparently limited, as the unit appeared in the catalog for only one year. *(M.L. Powell photo, Joe Piersen collection)*

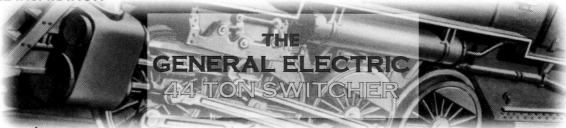

THE GENERAL ELECTRIC
44 TON SWITCHER

A number of railroads sought to take advantage of a 1937 railroad labor agreement that allowed the one-man operation of a diesel locomotive that weighed less than 45 tons. In 1940, General Electric responded to this demand and introduced a standardized model that met the agreement's requirements, the 44 ton switcher. These diminutive engines proved to be reliable, easy to maintain and, because they were lighter than most of the freight cars that they hauled, could operate over light rail and fragile bridges. Over 300 units were sold to Class I and shortline railroads, industries and contractors during the following 15 years. The center cab units were powered by small 190 h.p. Caterpillar V-8 diesel engines mounted inside each of the two hoods. Through the years, there were model variations in radiator and hood vent locations and the units' length varied from 31 to 34 feet (about 8 inches in "O" gauge scale). Many of these diminutive switchers worked the industrial areas of cities where the track was set in the pavement similarly to street car lines and freight cars would be switched alongside or directly into buildings such as factories or warehouses. The curves in these areas were extremely sharp and specially fabricated extensions of the couplers and air brake hoses were often needed to get the engine and freight cars around them. The *Pennsy Diesel Years* series of Morning Sun Books shows interesting photos of these units in such service. This is one area where an operator of Lionel trains could use "027" or "O"

gauge curved track on a layout and be completely consistent with the pattern of the prototype railroads.

In 1956, Lionel introduced its version of the G.E. "44 Tonner", as catalog No. 627 in Lehigh Valley lettering and a solid bright red plastic body shell and black sheet metal frame. This model used slightly modified components of Lionel's mid-1950's economy model of the 1000 H.P. EMD NW2 diesel switcher, including its power truck and sheet metal frame. Consequently, the unit was considerably oversized, resembling the much larger General Electric 90 or 100 ton switchers more than the better known 44 ton unit. A scale model of the 44 ton switcher should actually be closer in size to the small motorized units like the No. 41 Army switcher or the No. 53 Rio Grande snowplow. The prototype 44 ton unit had small drive wheels and a truck wheelbase of only 6 feet, 8 inches, compared with the 8 foot wheelbase of an EMD switcher. The cost of specialized tooling for a model like this was probably prohibitive in view of the modest sales volume that could be realistically expected. The unit did not possess the glamour of an F3 or Train Master, so Lionel understandably planned its production as economically as possible.

Lionel also produced a Northern Pacific "44 tonner" in 1956 as catalog No. 628 with a black body shell on a yellow painted sheet metal frame as well as a Burlington unit, No. 629 with a silver body and red frame. In 1957, the Lehigh Valley center cab switcher reappeared as No. 625 in a black and red color scheme along with a new addition, the No. 626 Baltimore & Ohio with a blue body and yellow floor. In addition to being grossly oversized, these models generally carried color schemes that bore little resemblance to anything that appeared on the respective real railroads' rosters. With the recent introduction of highly realistic models of larger road units by Lionel as well as competitive manufacturers, we might still see a properly scale-sized model of this highly interesting locomotive that proved to fill an important niche among the country's railroads.

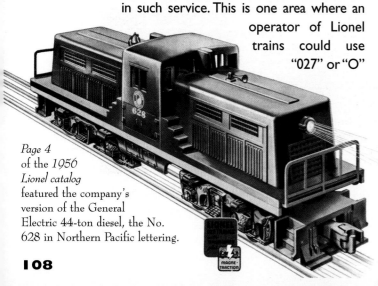

Page 4 of the *1956 Lionel catalog* featured the company's version of the General Electric 44-ton diesel, the No. 628 in Northern Pacific lettering.

In April 1964 at Oak Island yard in Newark, New Jersey, Lehigh Valley 44 ton switcher 60 awaits its impending sale to a Canadian limestone quarry. This is one real locomotive that could easily traverse the prototype equivalent of "027" track in tightly cramped yards along waterfront or industrial areas. (Gerald H. Landau photo, Matthew J. Herson, Jr. collection)

The largest railroad in the United States, the Pennsylvania, rostered 47 General Electric 44 ton diesels, one of which, the 9321 awaited the attention of shop forces at the Meadows Yard at Kearny, New Jersey in October 1960. (William J. Brennan photo)

The diminutive diesel switcher found a place on many Class 1 carriers' locomotive rosters as shop engines, on branch lines or congested industrial areas. New Haven was no exception, as it rostered 19 of the units, the last of which, 0818 pulled a wire train in 1950. (Steve Bogan photo)

SELF PROPELLED UNITS

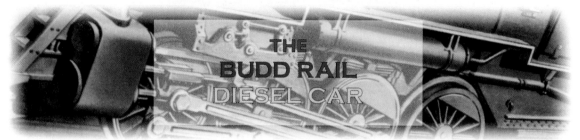

THE BUDD RAIL DIESEL CAR

I n 1950, the Budd Company of Philadelphia introduced its line of air conditioned stainless steel Rail Diesel Cars in four body variations ranging from the 85 foot long coach, RDC-1 to the 73 foot Baggage/Railway Post Office combine RDC-4. Each of the cars were propelled by two 275 hp General Motors Detroit type 2 diesel bus engines having six 71 cubic inch cylinders that powered the inboard axles through automotive design drive shafts and torque converters. The cars proved to be extremely popular as they offered air conditioning and other desirable amenities for passengers along with even better economy than the earlier decades' gasoline/electric self-propelled rail cars. They substantially reduced the operating costs of branch lines, shuttles and other limited volume passenger operations.

Lionel decided to produce its model of the Budd RDC car in 1956 as the powered coach No. 400, lettered for the Baltimore & Ohio Railroad. That road used the cars for commuter and intermediate distance passenger service. In the following year a three car train was offered with a powered RDC-4 Baggage/Railway Post Office combine as No. 404 with two No. 2559 coach trailers. A variation also appeared in 1958, the last year of production, with a powered No. 400 coach with a No. 2550 combine trailer and a No.

2559 coach trailer. The carbodies were fairly accurately reproduced in injection molded plastic, foreshortened to about 60 scale feet in deference to the sharp curves over which they were designed to operate. For production economic reasons, the company chose to use its existing GP7 power and trailing trucks that elevated the carbody somewhat higher than would be the case for an accurately scaled RDC. This use of a proven Magne-Traction power truck, however, enabled a single motored power car to pull two non-powered trailers.

A train of PRSL stainless steel Budd RDC-1's enter Wildwood, New Jersey to pick up plenty of passengers in 1955. The Pennsylvania-Reading Seashore Line was formed by PRR and Reading in the early 1930's to consolidate their redundant Southern New Jersey lines. *(Frank Watson photo)*

A brand new RDC-1 poses at Springfield, Massachusetts in April 1950 in a New York Central publicity photo. Most of these stainless steel beauties operated in suburban service near large cities, where they were visible to a large portion of the country's population. Consequently, the cars were a successful addition to the Lionel line and several variations appeared in the catalogs from 1956 through 1958. *(Ed Nowak photo, Morning Sun Books©)*

Lionel's No. 400 Budd RDC cars appear on
Page 27 of the *1956 catalog.*

THE "BURRO" CRANE

The development of self-propelled diesel cranes in a range of sizes enabled the railroads to perform track work and other light maintenance far more economically than using locomotive-hauled work trains. The most popular of the light duty models was the "Burro", which appeared on the rosters of many railroads. For example, one model with a 35 foot boom could lift a little over one ton at full extension, but up to seven and one-half tons at a ten foot radius. Understandably, these diminutive but versatile machines became quite popular with railroads across the nation. The visibility of these cranes, with the many operating possibilities, inspired Lionel to produce its highly animated No. 3360 "Burro Crane". The model also contains gearshifts that can engage the motor to raise or lower the hook or swivel the cab over an arc of about 300 degrees. It could be pulled as a crane car in a work train or propel itself with one or two cars. The author has often operated his "Burro" with a gondola and caboose as a fairly realistic light track maintenance train much like the photograph below.

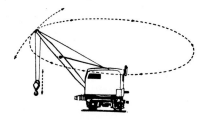

A Pennsylvania "Burro" crane pursues its light maintenance duties at Harrison, New Jersey in December 1968. The crane could pick up track parts, signal and interlocking machinery or any of a thousand heavy items along the right-of-way. *(Richard S. Short photo)*

The Burro crane was a popular piece of equipment on many US railroads. Often working with a minimum of ownership markings they usually always had that tell-tale "Burro" sign and yellow paint. This is Rio Grande #580 at Burnham Shop in Denver in September 1978. The 12 1/2 ton Model 40 crane was assigned to the rail laying gang RL5 which is stenciled on the side door. (John Tudek)

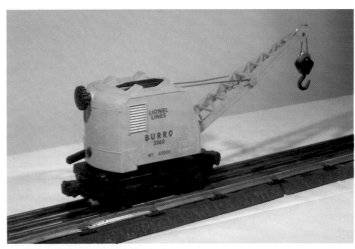

The illustration on page 29 of the 1956 Lionel catalog as well as the photographs of the author's No. 3360 "Burro" crane shows that the model captures the essence of the versatile prototype.

MISCELLANEOUS EQUIPMENT

DELUXE ALUMINUM PASSENGER CARS

The streamlining trend that started with the articulated PIONEER ZEPHYR and the M10000, which offered limited seating capacity, expanded to new versions of locomotive-hauled passenger cars in the years immediately preceding World War II. Resistance spot welding rendered stainless steel equipment economical to fabricate, as the metal's hardness and structural strength makes it more difficult to cut, drill or machine than carbon steel. The Budd Company of Philadelphia pioneered the technique which greatly reduced the need for mechanical cutting and fastening, but it was quickly adopted by other carbuilders as well.

The silvery sleepers, diners, coaches and other cars began to proliferate on the Burlington, Santa Fe, Seaboard and other railroads intent on improving the image of their premier passenger trains. The EMPIRE STATE EXPRESS of the New York Central appeared in stainless steel that extended to the trim on the streamlined "Hudson", and made its first publicity runs on Pearl Harbor Day, December 7, 1941. The streamlining of America's passenger trains would pause in deference to the war effort.

When peace returned, the railroads optimistically modernized their long distance passenger trains, usually with stainless steel cars. Lionel's marketing staff observed the trend and introduced a series of smooth sided plastic "027" sized passenger cars in 1948 and continued to produce them until 1966. The small plastic cars blended well with the smaller locomotives but, apparently, something more impressive was needed to accompany the elegant Santa Fe F3's which were essentially of full "O" scale size.

In 1952, the legendary 15 inch long 2500 series extruded aluminum passenger cars appeared in the catalog and were indeed eye-catching in real life. The sleek bodies were complemented with detailed die-cast

This drumhead sign graced the end of the Santa Fe's streamliner that operated between Chicago and Los Angeles, California. It and the Santa Fe SUPER CHIEF can be accurately represented with Lionel models. *(Robert J. Yanosey collection)*

trucks, injection molded plastic ends and even included safety-tread embossed on the vestibule floors. Extruded aluminum was produced much like toothpaste squeezed from a tube and the technique came into extensive use on storm windows and doors. Lionel used the process quite successfully, using the Budd company cross section with two noticeable longitudinal ribs running down the roof. They were the largest "O" gauge passenger cars that the company ever made, a scale 60 feet long. The original offerings were pullmans, dome cars and boat tail observa-

tions, with a baggage car following in 1954.

The cross section was modified in 1955 by eliminating a few side ribs providing a 1/4 inch flat letterboard above the windows and a flat 5/32 inch belt rail area below the windows. This enabled the company to add Pennsylvania CONGRESSIONAL striping and later adapting the cars to the handsome Canadian Pacific color scheme with maroon stripes and gold lettering. The use of these passenger color schemes did much to create the "Golden Age", as so many collectors regard Lionel's production during the 1950's.

LIONEL GLEAMING FINISH STREAMLINED CARS

Detail of streamlined car trucks.

1954 Lionel Catalog, page 29

Typical of the thousands of stainless passenger cars that re-equipped the nation's passenger train after WWII, at its Chicago coach yards, with the YMCA in the background, Santa Fe sleeper *Regal Lake* is prepared for the next run in April 1970. *(Owen Leander photo, R.J. Yanosey collection)*

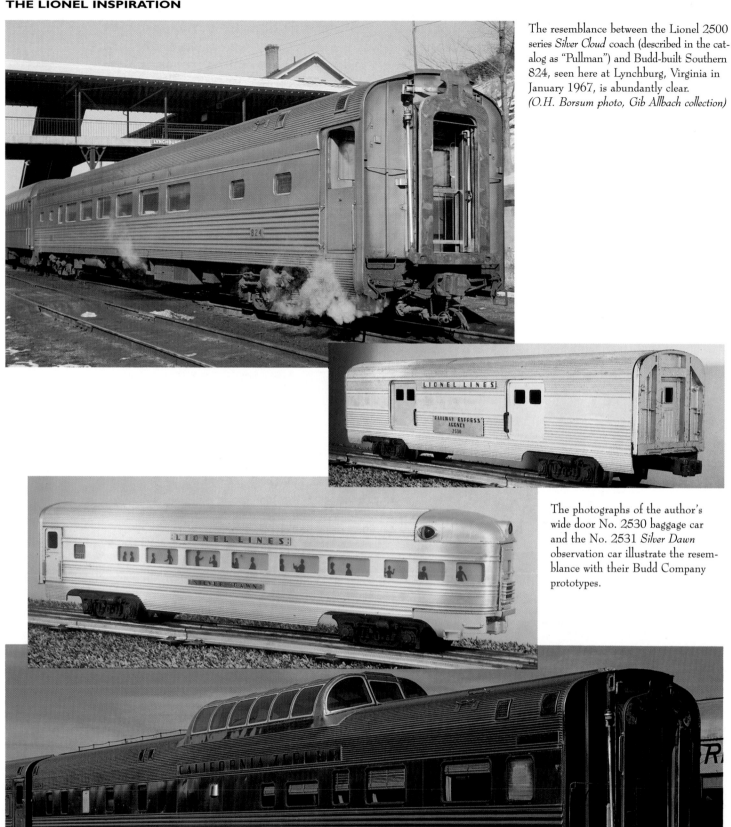

The resemblance between the Lionel 2500 series *Silver Cloud* coach (described in the catalog as "Pullman") and Budd-built Southern 824, seen here at Lynchburg, Virginia in January 1967, is abundantly clear. *(O.H. Borsum photo, Gib Allbach collection)*

The photographs of the author's wide door No. 2530 baggage car and the No. 2531 *Silver Dawn* observation car illustrate the resemblance with their Budd Company prototypes.

This view of Rio Grande Vista-Dome Dormitory-Buffet-Lounge 1140 *Silver Shop* shows how well Lionel adapted the design to its "Silver Range" dome car. *(John Tudek photo)*

Pennsylvania CONGRESSIONAL coach 1569, built by Budd in 1951 is seen at the Penn Coach Yard in Philadelphia, Pennsylvania in March 1963. *(William R. Martin photo)*

Lionel's quite realistic CONGRES-SIONAL cars are portrayed on *page 31* of the company's *1956 catalog.*

This view of sister car 1576 at New Haven, Connecticut in May 1959 shows the resemblance to the outline modeled by Lionel for its CONGRESSIONAL set. *(J.W. Swanberg photo)*

"MADISON" CARS

In 1941, Lionel introduced fairly well detailed models of typical 1920's or 30's heavyweight Pullman cars with molded Bakelite bodies and sheet metal floors and underframes. With the standard six wheel tinplate trucks of the period, the No. 2623 cars looked quite realistic despite being less than full scale size. They complemented the nearly-scale sized prewar "O" gauge steam locomotives like the No. 225 and 226 when operating on the 31 inch diameter curves of "O" gauge track. They were also large enough that they were not dwarfed by the scale sized No. 763 "Hudson" or its postwar counterpart, No. 773.

These elegant cars reappeared after World War II in 1946 and remained in the catalog until 1950. The postwar cars were painted in a shade of maroon that somewhat resembled the Tuscan Red passenger car color used by the Pennsylvania Railroad. The postwar trucks used a sheet metal inner frame with injection molded plastic detail overlays on the sideframes.

The cars were arranged much like day coaches in the sets in which they appeared. Prototype Pullman cars usually appeared on the railroads' premier trains and were almost always accompanied by dining cars, lounge cars and baggage cars. The author would have welcomed a series of companion cars in these formats, as was done later with the aluminum streamlined cars of the 50's.

The prototype passenger cars that most resemble Lionel's "Madison" cars, in the author's opinion, are the Tuscan Red sleeping cars and parlor cars operated by the Pennsylvania Railroad. An excellent example is Pennsylvania Parlor car 7001, *Courageous* at Paoli, Pennsylvania in January 1961. These cars were purchased by the railroad from the Pullman Company in December 1945. *(Frank Watson photo)*

PRR N5c
CABIN CAR

The Pennsylvania Railroad in the late 1930's and early 1940's was implementing modern styling created by Raymond Loewy and others on its electric and steam locomotives as well as some passenger train and station interiors and this carried over to the railroad's standard steel N5 cabin cars. The basic structure of the N5 that was designed in 1914 remained essentially the same but its external appearance was enhanced with an aerodynamic cupola and porthole windows in 1942. It created the "Buck Rogers" era N5c to blend esthetically with the experimental Q1 Duplex-Drive freight locomotive of the period.

In 1953, Lionel introduced its Catalog No. 6417 caboose in a close to full scale reproduction of the N5c with a quite realistic paint and lettering scheme on a painted plastic shell with sheet metal floor. It brought up the marker light end of most of the "O" Gauge freight train sets of that era, regardless of the type of motive power or its road name. With the artistic license typical of toy train manufacturers, the company produced the N5c briefly in maroon or gray with Lehigh Valley lettering (1954) and in blue and yellow with Virginian Railway (1958) lettering with a pastel version of the former bringing up the rear of the "Girls' Train" set of 1957-58. Despite the Lionel N5c approximately 10% reduction from full scale size, the author has observed many that were adapted for use on "O" gauge scale layouts, a compliment to the manufacturer's ability to capture the essence of the prototype.

Pennsylvania N5c cabin car (the railroad's term for caboose) 477926 poses for the camera at Sandusky, Ohio. With the exception of Lionel's omission of the rooftop train phone antenna, the 6417 is quite a good representation *(Emery Gulash photo)*

250-TON DERRICK AND BOOM

Railroads have used cranes and derricks of various capacities, ranging from "Burro" cranes used for light lifting associated with right of way repairs to massive 250 ton machines used to lift derailed locomotives. Until World War II, nearly all were steam powered but, as the railroads themselves converted from steam to diesel power to move trains, derricks, too, were diesel powered. Many old steam derricks were converted to diesel during those years.

In 1946, Lionel introduced its No. 2420 crane car, a scale proportioned, well detailed model of a Bucyrus Erie 250 ton derrick or wreck crane. The model is considerably smaller than a full scale model in deference to the less than scale sized locomotives and cars that would accompany it in train sets. Despite their reduced size, a few of these Lionel derricks have been modified and used on scale model railroads. The model had a plastic cab and boom, a die cast frame and rode on six wheel

Page 9 of the 1954 Lionel catalog shows the No. 6460 in a train set with its companion boom car.

trucks nearly identical to those used on the "Madison" Pullman cars.

From 1952 through 1954, the car used four wheel trucks identical to those used on Lionel's other freight cars and carried the number 6460. From 1955 to 1966, the frame and boom were black plastic and the cabs appeared in red or gray plastic. The change to four wheel trucks made these derricks more closely resemble the medium duty 150 ton machines used by many railroads. Because of the length of the boom, derricks were coupled to flat cars, gondola cars or specially designed boom cars to provide the necessary clearance. The prototype railroads often converted obsolete freight or passenger cars for this service. From 1946 to 1957 Lionel manufactured a boom car that represented a wood cab and tool boxes mounted on a steel flat car. The No. 2420 boom car had a plastic superstructure mounted on a die cast flat car. It was well proportioned and was an excellent match for the crane.

Denver & Rio Grande Western 250 ton derrick 028 was assigned to Grand Junction, Colorado when this photograph was taken in June 1975. The resemblance in overall apearance to the Lionel version is clear. *(Jim Sandrin photo)*

The pristine No. 2460 crane car in the author's collection represents a reproduction of the 250-ton Bucyrus-Erie derrick reduced to "027" size for compatibility with all of Lionel's locomotives and cars. *(William J. Brennan photo)*

The companion to Lionel's No. 2460 Crane Car was the No. 6420 Boom car, represented by this example from the author's collection. *(William J. Brennan photo)*

Although this is a smaller 120-ton crane, the boom of crane X23 and idler car X922 strongly resemble their Lionel counterparts. This scene was lensed in the NYC Mott Haven Yard in the Bronx in September 1958. The crane was used in the Park Avenue approach tunnels to Grand Central Terminal, thus the angled boom. *(Richard S. Short photo)*

THE LIONEL 6464 SERIES BOXCARS

During the time frame covered by this book, the boxcar was, by far, the most numerous of the varieties of freight cars moving the various products of farms, factories, mines, quarries and other cargoes. The burgeoning array of bright colors that began to decorate so many real railroads' box cars during the late forties and fifties, allowed the Lionel's art designers free rein and

most of the over 30 varieties of 6464's followed their prototypes' color schemes quite accurately. Unlike GG1's, Hudsons or Hiawatha locomotives, which could have their appeal limited by the actual exposure of their regional prototypes to Lionel purchasers, freight cars had a distinct advantage in that they roamed the entire nation. Thus, it was quite reasonable to assume that a prospective

Nearly new Boston & Maine PS-1 box car 76032 poses for the camera at New Bedford, Massachusetts in April 1957. One can see that Lionel's No. 6464-475, produced intermittently from 1957 to 1968, was a reasonably close reproduction. *(William T. Clynes photo)*

The 1954 Lionel catalog offered a tempting array of nearly scale sized 6464 series box cars including these that appeared on pages 32 and 33.

Lionel customer in San Diego could have seen a Rutland box car and a model railroader in Pittsburgh could have the opportunity to admire the striking "Rides Like a Feather" color scheme of a Western Pacific box car. This would work to Lionel's advantage in marketing over 30 varieties of colorful "6464" series box cars that it made between 1953 and 1969. The cars were nearly scale in size, about nine inches long. This compromise was apparently needed to render these colorful and fairly realistic cars compatible with the range of locomotives from small "027" steam locomotives to the full scale Train Masters.

As the selection of prototype box car photos indicates, Lionel's designers made good use of the available mass production lettering techniques such as rubber stamps, decals and hot stamping to achieve excellent likenesses of these colorful cars.

Baltimore & Ohio "Sentinel" 466032 was photographed at Council Bluffs, Iowa in November, 1954. Lionel's No. 6464-325 box car, which appeared only in 1956, strongly resembled its colorful prototype. *(Lou Schmitz photo)*

The Lionel 6464-175 all-silver Rock Island box was undoubtedly copied from the ten all-aluminum express box-cars of the 20060-20069 series purchased by Rock Island in 1945. These cars were used at first in express/passenger train service then later entered the general service freight pool photographed at Blue Island, IL in May 1967 near the end of its career. *(Paul Hunnell photo)*

New York Central's Jade Green box car 177769 illustrates the railroad's efforts at creating a new, progressive image at Battle Creek, Michigan in June 1959. Lionel got on the bandwagon with its No. 6464-900, which was introduced in 1960 and remained intermittently in the catalog until 1966. *(Emery Gulash photo)*

The 6464-375 Central of Georgia was offered by Lionel in 1956 and 1957 (reintroduced in 1966). The "watermelon" paint design, "Right Way" slogan, and yellow CofG logo were captured quite accurately by Lionel.
(Lou Schmitz photo)

The Lionel 6464-150 Missouri Pacific car was produced 1954-1955 and again in 1957 in many variations. For those collectors of the "Eagle" car variations, here is what the actual prototype looked like: MP Merchandise boxcar 46960 at Omaha, Nebraska on January 30, 1954. *(Lou Schmitz photo)*

A string of newly-rebuilt and freshly-painted New Haven boxcars return to service at New Bedford, Massachusetts in October 1956. Lionel's version, No. 6464-725 was a fairly late entry, being introduced in 1960, appearing until 1968, with the exception of 1967. *(William T. Clynes photo)*

Baltimore & Ohio developed a colorful scheme for the box cars dedicated to its "Time Saver" service. An example passes through Attleboro, Massachusetts on a New Haven freight train. *(Bob's photos)*

Some of the hardest-to-find 6464 variations are the 6464-300 Rutland. This is one of the many PS-1 boxcars which Rutland accepted delivery of in the mid-1950's. Rutland #145 was built in 1954 and photographed a year later in 1955 (at Council Bluffs, IA) the same year Lionel began making models of the car. *(Lou Schmitz photo)*

This view of New York Central's "Pacemaker" box car in Manhattan's 33rd Street yard in March 1949 illustrates how faithfully Lionel reproduced the colors and lettering patterns of the prototype. The Lionel "Pacemaker" was 6464-125 made 1954-1956. *(Ed Nowak photo, Morning Sun Books©)*

Lionel's No. 6464-650 (1957-58) Rio Grande box car was, within mass produced train limitations, an accurate presentation of its colorful prototype, seen here on May 1, 1965 at Council Bluffs, Iowa. *(Lou Schmitz photo)*

Pennsylvania 568169 wears the "Merchandise Service" color scheme in a service intended to compete with trucking companies on a speed basis. While Lionel produced several "Merchandise" cars before and after World War II, the company unfortunately (in the author's opinion) never used this attractive color scheme on any of these models. The car was photographed at Council Bluffs, Iowa in 1955. *(Lou Schmitz photo)*

THE CONCLUSION

The fifties would prove to be a "Golden Decade" for Lionel both financially and in terms of the variety and quality of the locomotives, cars and accessories that its catalogs offered. Joshua Lionel Cowan, the company's founder, retired in 1958 and many of his "first string" team had retired or passed away during that decade. The marketing, design and construction staff that succeeded them were apparently not as talented, so the quality of the trains suffered. As the sixties progressed, the fortunes of Lionel electric trains declined much in the manner of many real railroads. The public seemed to have lost interest in the electric train set as a major play item for children or a hobby for adults. After 69 years of production of electric trains in 2 7/8 inch gauge, Standard gauge (2 1/8 inch), "O" gauge, "OO" gauge and, finally "HO" gauge, the original Lionel Corporation ceased train production. The final catalog of 1969 was a skeletal six pages primarily advertising a series of budget priced "O27" locomotives and train sets, with a page devoted to "Famous-Name" 6464 series box cars. A small emblem on the cover commemorated the Golden Spike Centennial, the completion of the transcontinental railroad in 1869.

The author, like most Americans of the time, had Lionel trains as a youth but enjoyed a brief flirtation with "HO" gauge as a college student. He rediscovered the company's better prewar and postwar "O" gauge products during the 1960's at swap meets sponsored by the Train Collectors Association (TCA) and others. By the end of that decade, many "O" gauge scale modelers, who also frequented these events, expressed the opinion that the traditional a.c. powered "O" gauge trains operating on tubular three rail track would fade into extinction. Still possessing an RW transformer and an ample supply of "O" gauge track and switches, the author gradually accumulated a modest collection of Train Masters, F3's, GP7's and a 773 Hudson, which offered a quite realistic alternative to converting to "O" gauge scale two rail d.c. The train meets continued to proliferate along with the attendees and the membership in the TCA and other collector clubs mushroomed. The future would prove to be more promising than anyone ever expected at the time.

By the early seventies, the rising prices on prewar and postwar Lionel trains reached the point that production of new Lionel trains became economically feasible. A subsidiary of General Mills, Model Products Corp. (MPC), reintroduced many Lionel postwar steam and diesel locomotives and cars in new color schemes and created many colorful new products. New techniques in painting and lettering greatly enhanced the appearance of these MPC trains. A corollary benefit was the availability of many parts that had previously been difficult or impossible to obtain. In addition, the increasing values of certain highly desirable prewar items led some entrepreneurs to manufacture reproduction Standard and "O" gauge tinplate locomotives and cars. The world of Lionel trains was indeed reviving.

The 1985 acquisition of the Lionel line by

Richard Kughn under the name Lionel Trains, Inc. (LTI) brought what the author considers to be a new "Golden Age" for those who are familiar with real trains and who photograph and read illustrated books on the subject. The magnificent full scale sized Reading T-1 4-8-4, whose prototype the author saw and photographed on many occasions, was a "must have" item when it appeared in late 1989. The succeeding models, like the New York Central Mohawk, the new 700E and the massive full scale Pennsylvania S-2 steam turbine, were equally welcome in the author's collection.

In October 1995, Mr. Kughn sold the company to Wellspring Associates L.L.C. (Martin S. Davis and Greg Feldman) and musician Neil Young. They renamed the company Lionel L.L.C. It is most encouraging to see an increasing variety of vintage and contemporary prototype trains appear in the new Lionel catalogs in the form of high quality, accurately detailed scale models. To Lionel L.L.C. - Keep up the good work!

William J. Brennan
TCA #65-1344

The 1931 Lionel catalog had a cover illustrating New York Central engineer Bob Butterfield in front of the drivers of his Hudson showing a new 400 E model steamer to two young boys. Seventeen years later in 1948, and continuing for eight years, the Lionel Company began production of another one of its most famous models, the NYC F3. In 1950 the Lionel publicity department wanted a photograph of a boy beside a real NYC diesel in order to run it in an ad showing him playing with his Lionel model. On January 13, 1951, NYC company photographer, Ed Nowak, arranged to shoot the scene at Harmon, NY. With freshly-shined shoes and wide eyes, the young model railroader stood in awe of the fabled engineer and his trusty steed. What little boy wouldn't want to go home and recreate this wonderful moment with a No. 2344 NYC F3. *(Ed Nowak photo, Morning Sun Books©)*